THIS BOOK IS MY GIFT TO KAREN AS KAREN IS A GIFT TO THIS WORLD.

26MAR07

SPIRIT HOUSE
THE COMPASS OF CONNECTIONS

By

Charles E. Guffey

Published by
Sonnenschein Books
San Diego, California
First Edition, 2002
An Imprint of
Black Forest Press

"My music comes from a power beyond myself, it is not from my mind. My music is from heaven; it goes through my body and out my fingers when I compose. The songs I write are not my songs, they are music for everyone. So is this book, it is not Charles Guffey's book, it is a book for everyone and his writing comes from a power beyond himself. His writing, like my music, is one for all mankind to enjoy and appreciate - it is his gift for everyone, as are my songs."

Kitaro

SPIRIT HOUSE
THE COMPASS OF CONNECTIONS

By

Charles E. Guffey

Published in the United States of America
By
Black Forest Press
P.O. Box 6342
Chula Vista, CA 91909-6342
800-451-9404

Cover Design: Dahk Knox

Disclaimer

This document is an original work of the author. It may include reference to information commonly known or freely available to the general public. Any resemblance to other published information is purely coincidental. The author has in no way attempted to use material not of his own origination. Black Forest Press disclaims any association with or responsibility for the ideas, opinions or facts as expressed by the author of this book.

Printed in the United State of America
Library of Congress
Cataloging-in-Publication

ISBN: 1-58275-131-5
Copyright: August 2002 by Charles E. Guffey

All rights reserved

The Messenger

One came upon him not too late
just in time to meditate.
Immersed in angelic harmonies
of the spheres.
Realizing this *Heaven and Earth*
must be shared
with souls of spiritual children everywhere.

Charles E. Guffey, 1998

Publisher's Note: All of Kitaro's musical album composition names and record titles have been italicized for special emphasis. Example above: *Heaven and Earth*

THE MESSENGER

Table of Contents

FOREWORD

Dedicated to the thousands of people who created the magical meeting place. Doubt if worthy of task. Purpose. Exercising honesty and truthfulness with constant and careful attention. My judge and knower. Sharing with those who do not know.

PREFACE   Page vii

CHAPTER 1   INTRODUCTION   Page 1
How the *Innocent People* were embraced *From The Heart*. Responsible artisans. Introduction to Kitaro and saturation of his wordless musical vibrations. An illusionary crisis. Music identified. Health benefits, happiness and increased spiritual understanding. Two fold purpose: My education and most importantly theirs. Developed real musical appreciation.

CHAPTER 2   PERSONAL BACKGROUND   Page 3
Home and family. Mentally. Spiritually. Financially. Socially. Physically. Fear of poverty, criticism, ill health, loss of a loved one, old age, stagnation and death. Tests, trials and self-imposed hardships. Limitations. The Phoenix. Molded into compromises. Relationships. Mainstream. Kathy's clown. No musical appreciation. Special thanks.

CHAPTER 3   THE TOURIST SHOP   Page 7
The world came to me. In the beginning all was not good. Alchemy. Patience, simplicity and compassion. Opening. Progression. Observing and listening. *Time*. Guided by forces.

Stream of Beings. Unusual meetings. Witness. Graced with another important discovery. Gates of knowledge. Stranger inside. Months of research. To be, or not to be, that is the question? Alone with Kitaro. Synchronicity? Conventional paths not followed. Accurate presentation. Magical meeting place.

CHAPTER 4   THE MESSENGER   Page 23
Preserving Kitaro's privacy through essential published materials. A much happy man. Well done is better than well said. Feelings. Spiritual Bridge. Picture music. Enlightened beings. Music-background to a mental picture. Listening. Poetry. Nature speaks through Kitaro. "I put a lot of air into my music." A collection of the major printed material published by record companies and other media forms about Kitaro. More important messages from Kitaro.

CHAPTER 5   RESEARCH   Page 35
Patrons mandate Kitaro's music. Album titles and sound tracks. Continued research. Kitaro's music availability. Travels to search-out Kitaro's music. A taste of definitions. The Laboratory.

CHAPTER 6   THE DECISION   Page 41
For the benefit of the *Innocent People*. Begin to begin. The world as my stage. A live orchestration. Presented with passion. The ultimate self-assignment.

CHAPTER 7   SPIRIT HOUSE   Page 43
Tourist shop transcended to Spirit House. Music of the Spheres. Recognizing a unique opportunity to further self-knowledge. *Time* and space. Music could be mightier than the written word. Touched by the angels. Please help me. Discovering self. Right livelihood. Safe zone from chaos. See no evil, hear no evil and speak no evil. An undistorted view and cross section of the

many faces of humanity. Cycle begins again, the children. *A Passage Of Life*. Spirit House destined to dissolve and disappear. *Nageki*.

CHAPTER 8   RESPONSE   Page 51
The realm of *Kitaro's World of Music* and *The World of Kitaro*. From Russia with love. People with a particular need or want. Synthesized lives. A close encounter of the third kind / meeting Kitaro. Continuous marathon of Kitaro's music. The Musician's struggles. Pulled and pushed to try other musicians. Professional contributors. Old Kitaro fans who got lost along The Way. Endless customer comments, feedback, confirmations, affirmations and testimonials. Music is too intrusive, relaxing, spooky or scary.

CHAPTER 9 PASSION, PULP AND PROFITS   Page 61
Without seeing darkness one could not recognize the *Light of the Spirit.* Rightness will show you the way. The lure and reward of money. Fringes of a personal error. Truth and Justice. www/computer. Highest reward. When the student is ready the messengers will appear.

CHAPTER 10   THE JOURNEY: A RECAPITULATION
INTEGRATING The "JAPANESE CONNECTION." Page 67
"There is no beginning and there is no end." Manifestations of fluttering butterflies. Spiritual stimulation. Energy of Spirit House shifted again. Voyage of self-knowledge. To be continued.

PREFACE

This narrative is a chronicle of special moments in our *Time* shared with the many messengers of this *Planet* from a meeting place prearranged for them, and myself.

It all began with my desire for more self-knowledge when I was placed into an alien business environment and resigned myself to minimum compensation, initial confrontations, obstacles and hardships. This situation was to yield mutual repayments on a personal and collective level for all those that came in contact with it as the benefactors.

Within a few years, I made a most timely discovery that was helping me along the way, that had been the missing ingredient. A responsible musician, *Kitaro's World Of Music*, with a career of unprecedented accomplishments spanning over thirty years named, "A Much Happy Man" and labeled a "Spiritual bridge" that became a major contributor to the needs of many.

My *Journey* had now progressed so far. It has gone from a personal agenda for a self-serving purpose, to a plan to stimulate and awaken some from their *Endless Dreamy World,* reminding them to become responsible for their own actions through balancing their feelings and desires and by sharing, with others, what we all will eventually be aware of; *Peace Through Kindness* brings *Peace on Earth.*

I had also made another discovery that I could isolate myself in my studies while performing on this world stage and have reserve energy to help some along their way. These events could have never occurred in the insulated plastic corporate world from which I came, hiding behind a desk with the illusion of a cubical commander performing tasks for worldly mass destruction projects.

My proposed purpose progressed in a clear way on exactly what should be done and what should not be done. I only had mandates from the people, research and constant self-examinations; my plan plan would be to simply share the musical experiences I was encountering, with this *Magical Wave* of tourists, and provide a collection of published information on Kitaro for the benefit of anyone interested.

"I like to stay in nature, working, walking and learning."

Kitaro

DEDICATION

This book is first dedicated to the thousands upon thousands of wonderful people who I have had the opportunity and privilege to encounter from around our world. This began in 1993 and has continued into the *Millennia* in a very special sanctuary of peace and tranquility. These friends are truly the authors.

The only doubts experienced in the writing of these factual accounts are: would I be qualified for the task and should it be published, if so, for whom and what purpose, when and why? Although I had been requested, time after time by these visitors, to document these very wonderful and special events that touched so many spirits *From the Heart*. Also as hard as "I" tried "I" could not eliminate this personal pronoun due to interfacing directly with those thousands of contacts. Regardless, the foundation would be honesty and truthfulness coming assiduously from my heart. Eventually I would know what should be done or not done. But for now, I continue doing the very best with what I have to work with and use.

Above all, to my judge and knower, who guided and granted the competence and wisdom of *Cosmic Love* from the all encompassing universe which provided this form that houses the real me, the spirit, which is on a journey of eternal progression for the purpose of returning to perfection.

I do not claim to know anything, only to share what moves others and myself for the benefit of those who I feel do not know, and be aware of not becoming a prisoner of my own knowledge along the way. In conclusion, it should be noted that any knowledge discovered over these many years, in my quest,was obtained without a teacher or personal guru type, except for the essence of Kitaro's music, which liberated my thinking, and was solely acquired through extensive research and semi-isolation. I had truly become inebriated from my free spirit nature. Checks and balances are made to the best of my ability to confirm events of the now and so-called hereafter, as a novice. My only purpose was, is and always will be, *Thinking of You.*

CHAPTER ONE

INTRODUCTION

The information contained herein hopefully goes beyond recording the synchronicity of events, contacts encountered, spooky stuff, personalities or simply being an autobiography. It is how *Innocent People* were embraced *From the Heart* with some fear and suffering dissipated temporarily to lessen the massive self-imposed sufferings created over the years, from mundane existences early in their lives. This has been perpetuated along the way and justified by others and confirmed to themselves until they wake up from their sleep and see *The Light of the Spirit*.

The purpose of this commentary will be to share what is believed to be musical history, in the process of being revived by responsible artisans. They can lead any receptive person to a spiritual awareness and healing on their own *Astral Voyage*.

I was initially introduced to one responsible musician's music, in the fall of 1996, while operating my small tourist shop. Coinciding with our space and time, I was being confronted with what appeared to be a major personal crisis. As the situation progressed, I would saturate myself with this music day and night, becoming consumed by it and the crisis dissolved into the illusion it was. I had never heard such peaceful music with so much feeling in my life. A metamorphosis was occurring within me as quickly as the *Dawn / Rising Sun* of a new day. My attitude was becoming more focused on exactly "what I should hold onto" and "what I must let go of" became crystal clear. I was feeling compelled to share this music with all those I came in contact with, in a subtle and subliminal way. While the patrons did their shopping, my hopes were that they might feel a little peace before they went on their way, as I had. I never realized the full impact or potency of this music or that I would experience the accelerated growth I continue to experience today.

I have found the personal benefits of hearing, listening and feeling the breath of life from this music: it facilitates me being a much happier man while improving the four senses, enhancing memory and steadily developing music appreciation, and a quest for understanding every thing.

CHAPTER TWO

PERSONAL BACKGROUND

I was born in a small Indiana farm community during World War II, while my father was in a South Pacific Campaign. I am from Irish, Scottish and Cherokee Indian decent and was reared in what appeared to be a cultureless community of mundane existences stagnating and stifling with limited and biased views of our world and its inhabitants.

I was spiritually reduced to European puritan points of view without consideration for other faiths or ways of life and blended with heavy doses of hypocrisy. This all seemed very confusing to me as a child. But I did have a feeling for two things. When I did do something right it was *Heaven* and when I did something wrong it became hell.

However, during school vacation in the summer months, I would spend all my days alone at the local creek with the *Spirit Of Water* and with my dog and other animals and birds just relaxing in unbelievable *Peace*. Those periods of total isolation created a reference point I use even today when I require a little bliss in my life to feel the *Harmony Of The Forest*.

The home, family and social life situation was further compounded when we were infected with a rare decease, for that time, diagnosed as a broken home with all of its associated ailments. We were relatively poor but fortunately no one ever told us. But, my situation didn't present much in the way of constructive guidance from any peers or authority figures for further development, and I knew someday I would have to become responsible and change the course of my direction.

In that era, any exposure to culture (especially appreciation for music with depth and meaning from the old masters) was little to nonexistent. In those adolescent years, perhaps being preoccupied with fad music was the rage from artists who were here today and gone tomorrow.

Between the ages of sixteen and eighteen, I had managed to leave home in my 1951 Studebaker, quit high school and join the U.S. Air Force. I was discharged early and classified as unadaptable to military life. These early events obviously created some serious self-imposed sufferings that took years to overcome. Later in life, I discovered within that suffering is the seed for happiness and within happiness is the seed for suffering. But there were the benefits for learning the basic human fears of poverty, criticism, ill health, loss of a loved one, old age and death and how to overcome them. The primary lessons learned became invaluable: love and have respect for myself first, stop blaming others for the decisions I was making and manage my ego. Now I was beginning to understand that basically I was just responding to my unbalanced feelings and desires and allowing my own senses to react to things around me, which I had manifested, and they were not always what they appeared to be.

However, in my reality, I had placed myself in harms way and realized there had to be a major reversal in my attitude or I would be doomed to substandard survival. Having feelings for my potential inner growth, I became aware there was hope even with these illusions of limitations. As Frank Lloyd Wright stated in effect, "..some of man's greatest achievements were when he was faced with limitations.."   Illusion

By nineteen, I had acquired a decent position with a major aerospace company performing tasks on secret military projects which reflected the beginnings of self-worth and other personal benefits I had never envisioned. Only in America. Was this possible?

During those years, these state-of-the-art aerospace and ordnance manufacturing industries provided the specialized education, interactions and most importantly motivation for further education.

And let's not forget the sense of security. But, we were producing death machines with the potential of total destruction of the world and justifying this negative effort with politics, religious beliefs and economics at all levels.

Within a few short years, I had become more or less mainstream busy acquiring material things and fulfilling the American dream by manipulating and maneuvering myself and others for positions of responsibilities, social life, loan repayments, retirement incentives and other plans of grandeur. But it was a fight all the way to whatever accumulated advancements I had made with new homes, automobiles and credit cards. It wasn't working for me or on me, but for them. I realized I owed my soul to the company store. It seemed I was cursed with an abundance of ignorance and had managed to get myself wrapped around the axle of the world.

This material struggle creates and perpetuates a solid material world without any escape for the masses. A form of self-imposed entrapment or bondage was lured by my senses to get self-satisfaction for instant gratification. It was just an emptiness that couldn't be fulfilled after running the gamut and reaching a saturation point. I discovered I had a tendency to borrow money I didn't need, to buy things I really couldn't afford and to impress people I didn't know.

"Care about people's approval and you will be their prisoner." *Tao Te Ching*, Loa Tzu, 551-479 B.C.E.

Unhappily married with two beautiful children also qualified me for being molded into conformity, incompatibility and compromises to further stagnate and dim the twinkle in my star while looking for love in all the wrong places. I was trying my best in complying with and conforming to the needs and wants of others. Where did the *Dream* go? I had forgotten what was inside me.

Beginning in 1983, for seven years, I lived alone studying who, what, how, why and when I am. I had feelings I was the one dysfunctional all this time. I had actually fragmented myself into a multiplicity of "I's". I was the negotiator for subcontracts, I was a father, I was the husband, I was the groundskeeper, I was the investor and so on, with little to no time for the real me: my spirit.

Everything I had been doing was for the wrong reasons with the wrong people and at the wrong time, etc. I had actually used force to make everything work. I had learned as a sailplane pilot to manage all available energies to remain aloft. But I had failed to apply this basic technique in my daily affairs and it had all eventually imploded and vanished. Somewhere something went terribly wrong. It seemed I was learning all these lessons in life but was always given a new test along the way.

The key is practice-balancing feelings and desires with one's needs and wants regardless of what other people say, think or do. Simply resigning to counting your blessings for whatever you have is real wealth and peace. Then the continuous internal filmstrip and chatter will end the chase. It is similar to being satisfied with a manual toothbrush rather wanting an electric toothbrush. Both will do the job but one is much more costly.

In the event one cannot compromise, recognize the earth's population is polluted with ignorance's for satisfying personal needs and wants, and consideration should be given to the human and natural resources consumed to produce these things. In the recent past our consumption rate was being compounded, now the rate is exponential. For example, we will deplete the entire world's supply of oil in four hundred years that took mother earth (*Gaia*) millions of years to produce. This fact is no longer a debatable subject. Even with proposed alternatives there exists the age-old cause and effect reality.

"We should all respect nature, always". (*Gaia* – Kitaro 1998)

In conclusion, a special thanks to the many messengers along the way who have been a unique inspiration and an occasional reality shock; to the teachers of attachment and detachment for they are the true steppingstones along life's path. For without them, where's the reference point? In the end, they are just a reflection of me.

CHAPTER THREE

THE TOURIST SHOP

The world came to me and I greeted the world and the world allowed me to feel its pulse.

I had established a small retail shop, as a sole proprietor, in September 1993, located in Southern California, in the heart of a major tourist area that generates six million people annually *Westbound* from around this *Planet*. This store was originally named "Depot" and I subsequently changed it to "Connections" without any preconceived intent. Initially it had begun as an escape from high stress employment just to earn a living and attempt to discover some extension of *Peace*. I did not realize, at the time, this operation was not to find *Peace* for my personal welfare but for the public's and, in turn, it brought me more lasting *Peace* and happiness.

The store began with four wheeled pedal bikes, baby strollers and wheelchairs; it was a rental business. These bikes would accommodate two or more peddlers to self-tour this assumed historical area. Families would return, year after year, to peddle these carriages around. And the Mrs. America Pageantry rented the entire fleet for filming one day. I had even accumulated a collection of shoestrings, pants cuffs and panty hose that had been chopped off by the bike chains. I quickly became accustomed to endless waves of incoming and ebbing tourists and soon discovered there is nothing that compares to the smell of hotel soap on a tourist in the morning, the pain on their faces from new tennis shoes they had just purchased for their vacation and their confused look when the airlines informed them their luggage had been forwarded to Australia by mistake.

Later these rentals were blended with retail products when supporting the business solely from rental income became questionable. The bike rental portion of this business was labor intensive and, at times, became unpleasant and confrontational with some customers while working in an alleyway without a roof and without any normal facilities. For example, no restroom, one electrical outlet and one dripping faucet, and water ran through my place when it rained. Just to make it more interesting, the local police department constantly harassed me for parking the rental bikes on the public street. Fortunately the local fire department or building inspectors didn't arrive to look for the stealth construction techniques and the maze of creative electrical wiring networks. But the city did issue numerous city administrative citations for improper signage and other miscellaneous assumed infractions. The local residents and merchants had generated these complaints with their own self-serving agendas that could not be defended by me directly due to anonymous accusers. I had the distinct impression they were trying to run me out of town. Becoming anxious, I thought I would be forced into implementing Sun Tzu's two thousand year old *Art of War* techniques, but they were all overcome one by one when applying patience, simplicity and compassion. Regardless of the mission and subsequent adverse events I had to pioneer, a viable business still exists in that alleyway today, serving and entertaining the tourist who planned and saved their money to vacation here where no business had gone before.

Not accustomed to the overall crudeness of this type of operation, and the facilities, it all seemed to be a test or challenge for developing my equanimity whether or not it could be made into something worthwhile. However, the store did progress as additional unique and interesting items were being introduced originating from China, India, Egypt, Mexico with bronze statuary from Thailand. Also the working facility showed some improvement for creature comforts. I had tuned into a local jazz station to fill the place with music even though this music was generally repetitious, without substance and was boring, but at least the customers seemed to enjoy it. Most patrons found the place stimulating or overwhelming to the senses; one customer asked, "What is this place?" I told him it could be anything he wanted it to be and he quickly and quietly left.

In less than six months, the business was at least supporting itself. But my desire was not to become a merchant giving over my essence to a business just to earn a living. I often observed other shop owners rival between themselves and prostitute their businesses with insignificant products for the purpose of generating income for themselves and for their employees. This didn't seem too fulfilling for their owners or the patrons. It should be noted that small business seminars I attended projected that ninety percent of these start-up businesses would fail the first year. In actuality, ninety percent of that group have no business being in business. After observing many businesses, in this area come and go over the years, it appears that many novice entrepreneurs give ninety-nine percent inspiration and only one percent perspiration to their *Dream* of ego satisfaction, while searching for instant monetary satisfaction. I was left with a feeling that these visitors wanted more. But what was it? There had to be more to grasp. Being placed in this position wasn't by chance. Anyone, providing their heart is focused, could start and maintain a business and keep it running? However, there are better means of earning a living independent of an employee status. And there was the downside if I continued to follow my feelings just to earn a living, giving my all to the people, would leave me behind without a future retirement or dental plan and no gold watch at the end. I would be working without a safety net like performing on a *Solar Trapeze* as in *Cirque Ingenieux*.

Following four years at that location, a better location, and having a real roof, was secured only a half block away. It is adjacent to a saloon with the sound of the crack of queue balls echoing the general suffering of humanity. In one way, it was sad to be leaving, but I could take the memories of those who made it all possible. The rental bikes and a new thirty-dollar tarpaulin roof remained with the new owner at the old location for his… experiences! The operation continued again, at this new location, with refinements and streamlined only to coincide with the desire to provide an environment of tranquility for everyone who came in contact with it.

At this new location, the inventory was mixed with icons and images representing many different religions, faiths and means of spiritual understanding. Even a grand six foot tall bare-breasted bronze mermaid fountain, with a fishpond, graced the main entrance to the store, which became an instant qualifier whether to enter the store or not to enter the store. All these items became alive as a *Magical Wave* of customers flowed in and out. Watching and listening to their reactions provided further comprehension of our learned biased views. Although this is not a tourist trap, this store isn't for everyone. I was soon discovering if the store was selling anything at all, it was selling only feelings. And that was all. The products were only a guise.

Listening to customers became absolutely essential for how they expressed their feelings and desires in regards to the essence of the store. This provided me with more insight into further changes of products and displays. Taking in all their suggestions and digesting them became a rewarding and positive education. After all, in the end, it was for the benefit of their store.

The luxury of *Time* was never considered as an element working by oneself, but discovering that all past experiences had actually consumed *Time* of mostly inefficient ends, at the pleasure of someone else, or became non-fulfilling and was engulfed in a frenzy of manufactured *Time* constraints. Now was the moment to exercise the management of this manmade commodity to the fullest extent without regimentation or structure, but free flowing to nurture this enterprise into a more viable meeting place.

Being guided by forces to "know what to do" and "when to do them" became natural somehow. Was this based on my past experiences or intuitive nature, or were raw mental and physical forces pushing this business? It is not to say there were not struggles and challenges that would tax the patience of a saint but, sometimes waiting and doing nothing clears the muddy water.

I see *Time* on the faces of these visitors and hearing them say,

"We must leave now to catch our bus", "We are just killing *Time*" or "I can retire in just twelve more years from the phone company". Many of these retired people revealed to me when they were young, "They wanted to be or now that they're older, they used to be…" It appears very few ever realized exactly where they were in any given moment of their lives. Some realized they had become entrapped with financial obligations or were slaves to relatives with no escape for their personal lives and just earning a living on the treadmill of their lives as their clock ticks away *A Passage of Time*. They seem to forget or not know their true identity. Some would share their desire to change their lives from the slavery they had followed for years, in a *Dream* state of delusion, with *Nowhere To Land*. One patron, I had known for years, told me, "I just retired last week, and now I get to do what I want." My reply was, "You should have been doing that all along." A female police officer, from Los Angeles, cried as she told me her story of self-entrapment into the material world and financial obligations when all she really wanted was to raise her two babies. The self-imposed frustrations and sufferings are endless. As an *Ancient* philosopher implied, "First, one must realize he is in a prison before he can plan his escape." Who could not have empathy and compassion for these *Innocent People*? They are family. Perhaps their state was pre-arranged or controlled for the selfish gain of another, or not realizing they let others do these things to them. Or it is just something they had to work through in this lifetime?

Again this phenomena of our *Time* played an important part in this engagement, in that the hours I kept became insignificant and meaningless. That is, when the hour of the store opened or closed all ran together and became one as if the clock was an indicator of when the next flurry of contacts would be encountered for a mutual *Revelation*. Sleep or rest just became a necessary affliction to rejuvenate the body. However I had always managed to close the store, at the old location, for a typical afternoon nap in a hammock. And these breaks were continued at the new location also. On one occasion, I had forgotten to close the entrance to the old shop and was awakened in my hammock by three well-dressed men who asked, "Are you the owner"? They were CBS executives from New York City attending meetings in San Diego. One of them remarked as they left, "You know people would kill for a job like this." It is true; not being pulled by conventional family obligations or commitments, this dedication for exercising the right of being a free spirit is a luxury to some, but not in a selfish sense. The *Time* to contemplate, the *Time* to reason and the *Time* for self-knowledge should not be a luxury.

When the goal is to stay "in the moment", there is a *Time* to respond and a *Time* not to respond and a *Time* to do nothing. We have those choices. So-called free *Time* was commingled with work *Time* with play *Time* with vacation *Time,* etc, without differentiation and everything became fun, relaxing, entertaining and blended into a wholeness of being, by allowing events to occur around and through one with the least amount of meddling. At other times, I found myself just sitting here watching the wheels go round and round.

Periodically I would close the Tourist's Shop, post the gone fishing sign in the window and retreat to Japan, visiting historic temples and shrines. Once I was in the mountains of Japan, in the Kansai Perfecture at Koyasan, where no restaurants were immediately available. A Japanese family was kind enough to invite me to share their lunch with them that day. At another time in Ise, I couldn't locate my hotel late one night and a Japanese businessman took time-out to walk me there. What could I possibly do for him but thank him politely? By chance, while in Thailand, I met a retired Thai Army colonel and his family. They invited me to stay with them for a week. While visiting Bali, I witnessed traditional ceremonial cremations. Spontaneous experiences such as these are priceless and one could never have this degree of flexibility with regimented tour groups or conventional planning. This is quite different than the exposure I had experienced in this culture, to do this now, do that later, plan for this or that. Giving the moment our fullest and undivided attention is when others and we are the happiest; it is the only thing we have any degree of control over in this life.

However, comments are made when conventional paths are not complied with totally. Some would say, "You need a life." Who's? "What do you get out of it?" "You should do this or that." Why? There always seems to be someone lurking in the shadows ready, willing and able to manage our affairs, actions, thinking and destiny. But in the interim I did manage to rest when my body was tired, eat what and when I was hungry, drink when I was thirsty, work when I desired, think what I wanted and be with whom I wanted, etc. Liken to an uninhibited child, one might be inclined to say, I did it my way.

Perhaps I had exchanged from what was, to this minimum existence for maximum life experiences? The gap between my happiness and those who criticized this could only be measured in ignorance. I also became more aware of what was important to some people, was not important to me. What was becoming more important to me was not important to many. It's a lifestyle few could understand or have the desire to understand. For any worthwhile effort, applying our *Time* to our individual needs, plays an important part in gathering, assembling and assimilating data and only we, as individuals, know our own abilities to accomplish our duties. I had elected to use this commodity in exchange for these experiences that many could not possibly comprehend. How could they? They were wrapped-up tightly within themselves.

What was not initially realized, was that a *Stream of Beings* literally paraded through this *Oasis* from *Mother Earth* representing their customs, faiths and religions and cultures blended with individual personalities ready to share their *Chants from the Heart* beyond a superficial human exchange of verbal conversations in bearing their souls. And there were the ongoing conventions that sponsored continued education for professionals and special interests groups. The store was constantly revisited annually similar to a *Pilgrimage* of flocks of migrating birds in *Flight* to report back on their condition. Some would donate currency from their motherland for display in the sales counter, make entries in the guest book, forward gifts, thank you notes, letters, dinner invitations, phone calls and invitations to their homes around the world. Over the years, this ongoing collection grew into an array of mementos that continued to flow in from everywhere, but working single-handily, follow-up correspondence often became marginal due to the volume and obligations to my other duties. As one lady told me, "You have no one, but you have everyone."

Subsequently, as the store was progressing, a strange unexplainable feeling would make its presence that belonging in this situation of constant change and flux was similar to an *Ocean of Wisdom*. The exact reason wasn't realized at that *Time,* but it became crystal clear later that I required additional training and there was work to be done in this one-man university. I would just have to flow with the events unfolding around and through me; the performance must go on.

This author would witness or be directly involved with angelic and spiritual events and conversations from customers in unusual meetings, with complete revelations stating their personal happiness, sufferings or just general information. Learning to listen to them intently, with genuine concern, empathy and compassion, and learning to let go personally is just as important. Late one summer evening, when the store was packed with customers, an unidentified lady approached the sales counter in a precise manner and said, "I am here to help you get what you need..." and left. Who was she? These occurrences became so commonplace and pronounced I anticipated their next occurrence and believed this was typical. I would ask other shop owners if similar things were happening to them. Their replies were unanimously negative. Feeling out of sorts by even revealing these constant events and thinking perhaps the type of products I carried were generating or inducing these people to react in a way not ever experienced in life before. Of course, as the years went on, my acceptance level became so pronounced that looking forward to the next event became primary. There was information to be exchanged by the teacher or from the student that was necessary for both the participating messengers.

    Was I graced with another important discovery that was selected for me by chance? In the fall of 1996, after being given three cassettes of music by Kitaro, an artist I had never heard of before. This was exactly at the same point in *Time* an uncompromising individual, of a predator nature, initiated a legal confrontation with me. This confrontation of wrangling with attorneys, paperwork, delays, money and time consumed over one year of what appeared as a total waste of every resource on everyone's part, except for the attorneys involved. During that episode I continued running the business in an efficient manner. I cried to everyone, appealed to whomever for sympathy, but most importantly, maintained my sanity and accentuated my *Peace*. How could this be? The answer would lie in the facts. First, I was the one who placed myself in harm's way to become the victim again due to my latent insecurities. Second, I believed I already possessed the internal *Strength* to cope with almost any situation that could possibly arise. Third, Kitaro's music seemed to be from heaven and was allowing me to believe there was a force protecting and guiding me every step of the way. Was I special? I don't believe so. The positive work I had done on myself through the years was paying off when I needed it the most in possessing the right view. If all this were not the truth, I could have become mentally disabled as a human being and of no benefit to myself and certainly to no one else.

    During this era, my main goal was to research the stranger in myself, living in a mask of my worldly station to which I would apply some degree of austerity. This led me through many gates of knowledge and philosophy that I feel is only revealed, to a few who are clearly receptive. And once this course is pursued in earnest, with sincerity, every applicable piece of knowledge, needed at that point, will be revealed as one is ready to receive it through books, people or a divine personal guide. In regard to my investigation into Kitaro, this became an adventure. Not just to mimic what he had attained, but to acquire a working knowledge, and most importantly application, of exactly what all men with this ambition have been probing for and some had found it over the *Millennia*. What is it all about? Why the secrecy? Who or what holds the supreme knowledge? And would I have the mental horsepower to understand?

As a latecomer to the Kitaro Family in 1996, I first became aware of his music, twenty-five years after his musical career begun. His music shocked my spirit. It awakened the magic inside me and it put the twinkle back in my star. I would purchase whatever and as much as I could find, not knowing its content but believing all his music had to be of a beneficial nature. And it was and is. I could have never dreamed or expected to experience music with such a personal signature of penetrating power.

Even with my original primitive music equipment the store was filled with the messenger's heartbeat. Occasionally birds would come in and perch and listen. His heavenly music became dominant in the shop for over twelve hours a day, seven days a week. Customers would ask, "Do you sell this music?" At that time, I would send them away to a music store, but they would always return and inform me that they could not find his music or the selections were too small, or no one was willing to explain this extraordinary artist to them. These patrons would continually request that I carry Kitaro's complete collection. At that time, I did not feel this was something to just jump into. I needed a period for the right concentration. Kitaro's music was having an emotional affect on the people and I would be dealing with human psychology, and without a license? Who qualified me? Could this be a practical goal? My goal was to continue to expose his music and share my knowledge with those who showed an interest in him and his music, but this was not a music store, nor did I want it to become one. Also, I really didn't and don't know anything about music and my knowledge of current artists is nil.

Many months of diligent research was consumed in numerous retail music shops, locally and elsewhere, checking Kitaro availability of stock for new releases, category accessibility, available brochures, prices and personnel who could answer typical questions about Kitaro so I could get a feel for what the public would be

Spirit House

subjected to in advertisement. Generally what was found was only six to twelve albums were stocked that represented two to five albums. I found this to be a strange marketing situation for such an impressive artist. Only a true Kitaro follower, fan or fanatic would know what they were looking for, or even if it existed. Obviously Kitaro is not a mainstream artist for very good reasons. His music is spiritually awakening; seductive and penetrating to the soul and the typical run of human beings are not ready for that.

Not being qualified in marketing presented another question: by what method should the messenger's music be presented? That would be from a commercial approach and is exactly what should not be done. Furthermore, I had absolutely no desire to promote spiritual music sales through some funky little store that had been created by some off-the-wall musician. Kitaro's music is industrial strength and it wasn't just my opinion. The universe allowed me to see this far and now I must know what to do. If these patrons allowed me to give them an orientation and initially expose them to Kitaro would be most important to me. Whether they made a purchase or not should not be a concern of mine. If *Time*, condition and place were right, I felt it would all work out? From experience, I have always found a subtle approach solidifies a lasting impression of whatever one is trying to present and that would be my approach. Also, not everyone is ready to hear a message from any messenger.

From one point of view, it was to my benefit not to know anything of significant value about music other than it was pleasant or not pleasant. But after the benefits of hearing, listening and feeling the air of Kitaro's music I developed a musical rhythm I never new I had before. I had always been uncomfortable and avoided dancing with the girls' while growing-up and I couldn't tap my foot to music, much like Steve Martin portrayed in "The Jerk". But I seemed to be inspired to learn, in privacy, ancient and sacred dance routines to awaken the spiritual magic already existing in me. Also my memory and eyesight were improving. My hearing became more sensitive and my taste improved.

For me, these physical and spiritual experiences suggested to me this could be one of the fabled fountains of youth and it existed internally, not externally. But most importantly, his music was bringing more *Peace* and happiness to others and almost everything was more positive and solidified. I also desired to learn more of the mechanics of music and some of the great artists who create it. The world I had known was changing again and I wanted to share everything I was feeling and learning with others.

My favorite time came when I was alone with *A Drop Of Silence* in the company of the Master and his music. I can literally go anywhere I want and experience what I was truly meant to experience in this life… uninhibited feelings. I often reached a point where I didn't need his music. I could go beyond self-imposed limitations or reactions to my own senses into liquid stars and experience a degree of spiritual common sense of what I was capable of understanding from the breath of life. At times I felt everything until it dissipated back where it came from. I have always had this haunting awareness that perhaps I am special. In exactly what capacity, I do not know the question to this answer.

My other question would be why I wasn't aware that his music existed prior to 1996? And what was the cause for the synchronicity that most of his music being brought to my attention at exactly a point in *Time* that most of his albums were being consolidated from many record company labels, remastered, and put under the umbrella of one company in 1996? Who is the messenger or messengers? Why does he (Kitaro) have this connection with those who are ready for more self-knowledge? Why did his earlier fans abandon this inspiration for over-indulgences of the material world? There are many many more questions to be answered and some are not in my mind yet to ask. He deserves my total attention and dedication to properly represent him and his music. Also my orientation of Kitaro must be presented as accurately as possible to a potential customer, while at the same *Time* protecting his privacy. I could have never imagined the wonderful paths of joy and extension of my own personal development through which this crusade would guide me, and is still taking me. The performance at the

Tourist's Shop must go on.

THE MAGICAL MEETING PLACE

The World came to me, I greeted the World
And the World allowed me to feel its pulse.

Liken to a manifestation of fluttering butterflies,
Some would land and linger
To be caressed in their full beauty
And then released
Unharmed to continue their Sacred Journey.

Our Purpose fulfilled… for now.
Charles E. Guffey, 1998

CHAPTER FOUR

THE MESSENGER

First and foremost: my primary purpose is preserving Kitaro's privacy. And the second consideration is to provide some insight into the workings of The Messenger. The reader will come to his own conclusions, if any, without creating additional muddy water to wade through, but leaving him with his own feelings and interpretations without reading the script of another for his journey.

Prior to Kitaro becoming my self-appointed mission, I had already found him and his music labeled, mislabeled, lost in space, available in out of the way places, "wherehoused" in music stores, categorized and defined by the media and molded to conveniently fit a shaped form. You could find that he is consistent and persistent in relaying an enlightened message whether from dated material or most importantly from his music. There is no width, depth or length to Kitaro's music, it is just there, similar to the Universe. Resembling each one of us. There is neither a *Mysterious Island* nor shadows if one wishes to see.

"Whatever joy there is in this world all comes from desiring others to be happy, and whatever suffering there is in this world all comes from desiring myself to be happy." (Shantideva. Buddhist Monk at Nalanda University spanning the 7th and 8th centuries.)

Kitaro's Japanese nickname translates to "A much happy man."

As Benjamin Franklin stated in Poor Richards Almanac, "Well done is better than well said." This statement simply defines the results of Kitaro's wordless musical ability and the positive affects it has on people's lives from all walks of life from all around this *Planet* we call home. There are no metaphors like word-forms or labels to describe or define Kitaro or the music he produces.

Klaus Schultz, originator of the German musical group

Tangerine Dream and early teacher for Kitaro on keyboards said, "Music to me is the background to a mental picture, but the listener must make the exact interpretation, hence the music is only half composed and the listener himself should attack the composition to gain a mental repercussion. Some people don't invest effort into things if no material profit is to be had, unaware of the mental joys."

A famous guitarist once stated there is no obstacle between the instrument and the heart – only a slight layer of skin on the fingertips. And a philosophical writer stated, "Instrumental music is at best the harsh imitation or reflection of music of sound in space."

A select group of artists distinguishes their sensations, which belong to nature, from feelings, which are of themselves. They become sensitive to impressions from objects of nature and are moved to express them through poetry, music, painting, and other arts. As Kitaro continually states, "My ultimate goal is to keep expressing my feelings in music and for the people to enjoy it."

Throughout history there have been figures of artistic vision that have helped the human race to transcend. Tibetans Monks identify them as enlightened beings. And perhaps Kitaro is one of them. As we listen and feel Kitaro's music, it will remind us of our hidden wisdom nature more than what the spoken word could possibly relay.

His professional musical career now spans over thirty years and was initially dominant in Asia. He credits his ability to a higher source than just himself. For example he has stated, "This music is not from my mind. It is from heaven going through my body and out my fingers through composing." It is believed by some that the limitless power and variety of the rich music, produced by Kitaro, can be a visual and vibratory aid to enhance one's natural awakening if allowed to penetrate to the spirit. His music is a total expression of himself, his very being on this plane.

The following was taken from the *Best Of Ten Years* album insert (1976-1986), digitally remastered in 1996, and it continues to best describe Kitaro.

Long recognized as one of the most acclaimed recording artists in the Orient, Kitaro has always taken his music far beyond the boarders of his native Japan. As a composer and synthesist, he has reached millions of people on every continent with his stellar recordings.

Though his public presence has always been clocked in the tradition and mysticism of the culture into which he was born. Kitaro's music does not yield to boundaries or national categories.

Perhaps, as one-writer notes, it is his "Honesty and consistency that people seem to trust that keeps him in the forefront of modern music." It is, as another suggests, his compositions, which weave "A boundless play world of a thousand pictures... a web of gentleness and wonderment."

Since the early 70's, Kitaro's music has been a reflection of a consciousness which displays a reverence for nature and for the world as humanity's natural habitat. "Nature inspires me," he says. "To me, some songs are like clouds, some are like water."

The beauty of nature was part of Kitaro's earliest days. He was born (named Mansano Takahashi) to a Buddhist/Shintoist farming family in Toyohashi Perfecture, in central Japan in 1953, Kitaro grew up in bucolic isolation. The family grew vegetables purely for their own sustenance, and his rural youth gave him an early feel for the simplicity and grandeur of nature. "I found a place in nature when I was very young," He recalls. "And spiritually, I was always a Universalist in my outlook."

He came to music much later, as a high school student, when he discovered the electric guitar. Completely self-taught, he fell in love with American rhythm and blues. Kitaro says, "And I love classical music, which is like pictures, and rock music, to me, means power and energy. We have music so we can feel the universe." With some classmates, he formed a rock group named Albatross, which featured his early poetry set to music. "I was writing about my relationship with nature as a way to try to understand man's place in the scheme of things," he says. In the early 1970's, at which time he'd switched from guitar to keyboards, he recorded with a group called the Far East Family Band, as band members left from time to time, Kitaro would pick up their instruments; he taught himself to play each one. "By that time", " he recalls, "I had switched over to keyboards and we were doing a rough form of the kind of impressionistic music that I would later start playing." In 1972, Kitaro traveled to Europe, and during a recording session with the Family Band, met synthesist and Tangerine Dream founder Klaus Schultz. He listened and watched, and absorbed. He notes: "I became fascinated. I just kept staying with him longer, learning how to apply the synthesizer absorbing it all. When I returned to Japan, I started combining it with my own ideas."

That European encounter changed Kitaro's life and music. He stopped listening to other people's music and concentrated on refining his work with a variety of synthesizers. "I was playing around with it with my head headphones on and found that just moving the knob from left to right, I could create large and small waves. I could create an ocean, a whole scene – a winter coastline, a summer beach."

The Japanese were fascinated by Kitaro's music. The critics called it "sound pictures" and "mind music". "They had a hard time putting me into any category," Kitaro explains. "I'm a musician of the new culture. Japanese history and society is very colorful, very perfect, but in present day Japan, everything has been turned upside down to compete with Western societies. I wanted them to be reminded of things past whether they were individuals playing threw the stock market or farmers hoeing crops."

When Kitaro is working on his 32-track digital home studio, the windows are often open to the sounds of birds, wind and water (which often find their way directly onto his recordings). When he isn't recording, he likes to play football and raise horses. He also likes to build and set off fireworks. In fact, he is a licensed fireworks maker in Japan, and is expert in a type of display that is a specialty of his hometown. A large bamboo tube is filled with explosives and then tightly wound with rope. Pointed at the sky, it throws sparks 70 feet into the air, and since the cylinder is held close to the face, it must be handled very carefully. He hopes eventually to include the pyrotechnics in his concerts.

In Japan, he is considered a celebrity, with a reputation for being a reclusive, a kind of folk hero who blends the old with the new. "I give people privacy with my music," he says, "And they give me privacy in my life, I can come and go as I please without being bothered. I enjoy life to the fullest, but I think some people tend to see me as this guru-type figure, sitting up on the mountain in a lotus position, looking over the world."

For many years, a small and devoted audience in America, through albums imported from Japan and Europe, knew Kitaro. In 1985, that audience widened considerably when Geffen Records simultaneously released six compilations albums: *Asia, Astral Voyage, Full Moon Story, Millennia, India* and *Silver Cloud*. A seventh, *Toward the West*, was released shortly thereafter. Each of Kitaro's is developed around a specific theme or project. In 1980 he created the music to *Silk Road*, an hour long documentary about the overland trade route from Europe to Japan, which was produced by The Japanese National Television Network, NHK. The program was initially so well received that it evolved into a series that ran on Japanese television for five years. Kitaro's music for the series was released in Japan as a triple LP and appears in America and India.

The Theme from *Silk Road* is a highlight of his concert appearances in 1982; Kitaro scored the Toei science fiction animation film Queen Millenia, which is available on LP as *Millenia, Astral Voyage*; it is the story of a man in the universe; Full Moon Story is the results of Kitaro's contemplation of a single *Full Moon, Silver Cloud* which represents a period of reassessment during which he retreated to rural Japan, then emerged to work and compose.

Kitaro's 1984 Shanghai live recording album, *Asia* features a drum solo, a Kitaro hallmark. Every year for the last eleven years, at the first full moon in August, he plays huge Japanese ritual *wadaiko* drums at the foot of Mt. Fuji. The sessions lasts all night and into the morning. The drumsticks, big as baseball bats, are taped to his hands, which become bloody after hours of drumming. He has even passed out at times during these ceremonial evenings, only to revive and resume his drumming.

Kitaro conducts his ceremony, he says, out of gratitude, from a sense of appreciation for the mountain as guardian. The sprit in which Kitaro approaches this yearly event is a sign of his respect for nature, and it is no coincidence that members of American Indian Tribes, with whom he has become friendly, have joined him on such occasions. The "Wadaiko", which Kitaro calls his "Japanese Beast," can be heard for miles.

In 1986 came *Tenku,* Kitaro's first exclusive album for Geffen. The title, which means "Heavenly Sky", reflects the open-air environment of Kitaro's home studio. The album was made a two hundred year old farmhouse in the Japanese Alps. On the opening track, a child's laughter is heard. The albums theme concerns images and impressions of childhood.

In the fall of 1987, *The Light Of The Spirit* was released, co-produced with Grateful Dead percussionist Mickey Hart, a long time Kitaro admirer. Some of the recording was accomplished in Hart's native San Francisco, with an ensemble that included Pablo Cruise guitarist, vocalist Jeanie Tracy and percussionist Zakir Hussain. Thematically, *The Light of the Spirit* includes Kitaro's vision of life, death and rebirth, and continues his musical exploration of the life cycle that started with *Tenku.*

These sound images have been heard live by those who have attended Kitaro's concerts. During his 1984 Asia Tour, he became the first person to perform in both Taiwan and the People's Republic of China. It was during this tour that Asia was recorded. In 1985 and 1986, Kitaro undertook two major tours of Japan: The Yamaha Specials '85, and the Hen-Sei-Hu Tours in 1987, Kitaro toured the U.S. giving concerts in twenty-five cities in thirty-one days. He played to sold-out houses in many cities, including New York, Chicago, Boston, Los Angels and Atlanta, and was often required to add a second night to satisfy demand. A live recording made of one night's performance was later broadcast to stations around the country on National Public Radio. Kitaro's music fits into many of life's activities. In Japan, his records are played at parties: In America and elsewhere many use his music for meditation. He enjoys telling about the time, long before he became interested in music, when one of his teachers, a Zen Master, liked to call him Setu, a name that means bridge. The concert of a bridge, a musical connection between the East and the West, has occurred to many writers who have met and listened to Kitaro and his compositions. His music, though it has Japanese elements – notably the lovely and often intense sound of the shakuhachi, or bamboo flute – is universal in that it seems to reach past the ear and go directly to the heart.

The pulse beat inherent in many of his melodies is as much felt as it is heard. A young Japanese woman, after hearing one of the concerts on Kitaro's recent American tour, remarked to a bystander that, "...his music is like the heartbeat of an unborn child - you can feel it." Writers have hinted at the healing properties of his sound pictures, and Kitaro has acknowledged that his purpose is to calm the inner person. "The wars in the world don't come from outer space," he says. "People create them, people who have a war within themselves, I want to create music that eases that war within."

"I've traveled over India, Nepal and I've been able to make friends everywhere. My own peace comes from the realization that I am an equal of the beggar on the streets of Calcutta. Music has a transformation capacity. You can change a person's karma through music. I know it can change someone else's because it changes my own."

Kitaro is an original and universal soul who has become master of the wordless lyric and as he brings his music further into the forefront of American consciousness, there is no doubt of his growing popularity. In this 21st century, it's clear that music plays an important role in crossing barriers between cultures and societies. Kitaro's music, especially with its sense of peace and harmony with nature, will play a significant roll. He is indeed a bridge.

*"My music comes from nature--
almost one hundred percent."*
Kitaro

Kitaro's published poetry:

GREAT SPIRIT

ALL LIVING THINGS COME FACE TO FACE WITH THE
GREAT SPIRIT
AND THE GREAT SPIRIT DWELLS WITHIN ALL LIVING
THINGS
TREE FLOWER WATER WIND… ALL THINGS
AT TIMES THE GREAT SPIRIT IS SEVERE
AT TIMES THE GREAT SPIRIT IS SOOTHING
ENCOMPASSING ALL LIFE
EVERYPLACE OF THE GREAT SPIRIT DWELLS
IS THE SOURCE OF THE GENTLE CRYSTALLINE LIGHT
AND WITHIN THAT LIGHT WE BECOME ONE
FLOATING AS IIF IN OUR MOTHER'S WARM BODY
LIVING TOGETHER AS CHILDREN OF THE EARTH.
WITHOUT TIME
WITHOUT END…
By *Kitaro – Mandala 1994*

MESSAGE

I SEND A MESSAGE OF SOUND
TOWARD THE SKY
ENGULFING EMPTY SPACE
SOARING FAR BEYOND GRASP
HIGH ABOVE MOUNTAIN TOPS
BEYOND OCEAN WAVES
STRETCHING TO REACH THE ANDES
AND LIGHTLY TOUCHING NEPAL
WATCH AS THE SOUNDS FLOW
LISTEN AS YOU FEEL THE WIND BLOW
NATURE IS COLORED WITH ROMANCE
UNFOLDING A DRAMA DAY BY DAY
PLANTS BREATH A RHYTHM
INSECTS PLAY THEIR MELODY
LIGHT FLIES AS WIND CRIES
NOW CATCH THE SOUND... FEEL THE LIGHT
BY FEELING THINGS WHICH ARE WITH LIFE
INNOCENTS RESPOND TO THE DELICATE SIGH
OF THE WORLD, WEAVING THEIR OWN DREAMS
DREAMS WHICH SPREAD THROUGHOUT THE WORLD
PEOPLE BEGIN TO SING HARMONIES OF LOVE,
WORDLESS
THIS IS A BEGINNING
CONNECTING THE DREAM
TO THE COLOR OF YOUR BREATHLESS HEART
PEACE AND TRANQUILITY, YOU NEED ONLY TO SING
IT IS FOR YOU.
By ***Kitaro*** – *Tenku 1986*

As we could interpret, Kitaro's poetry is not restricted to one specific thought but encompasses all living entities that are woven together affecting a collective *Dream* reality by feelings we call nature. And it should be understood that we couldn't elaborate or speculate about another's essence, psyche, spirituality, etc. What can be presented with is a personal knowledge of Kitaro through his music and by his candid remarks quoted from different sources.

Kitaro's creativity, represented by spiritual dance movements, mudras, mantras, the mandala, poetry and especially his music is not the music of Kitaro in the conventional sense that the masses could typically have a deep interest in or understand. But he is the vehicle of transmitting the music for our benefit. This is not as strange as it seems. For example, Thomas Edison was questioned where he was getting all these thousands of ideas for his inventions and made a statement to the effect that his ideas came to him "out of the air". Edison was receptive to a higher power and was receiving specific information that mankind was ready for and he was only the energy transducer. Extensive open research has already documented such for those who have further interest. Sometimes we tend to think if it can't be touched or proven by scientific methods it's not real when in reality, the fact is, what we believe to be real, is the illusion. Therefore the majority of people are trained to regard only hard, coarse, physical and most material things and to hold them to be the realities. Unless you are a student of this philosophy it is to your advantage just to enjoy Kitaro's music, accept it if penetrates your spirit. Smile and learn from that point forward.

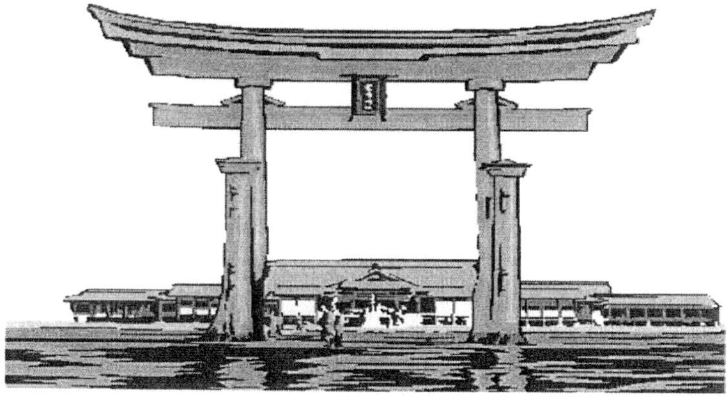

CHAPTER FIVE

RESEARCH: KITARO'S GATEWAY TO HEAVENLY MUSIC

Educating myself on Kitaro had become a primary task of tangible importance if the store were to represent him accurately and acceptably and make his complete works available to the audience. Initially his music was aired for personal pleasure and for the ambiance of the store, but now the patrons mandated supplying them with his music and more information about Kitaro the person.

I had now become convinced by an overwhelming cross section of people from around the world, to stock Kitaro's entire collection of music in The Tourist Shop. Any merchant could stock his music, and I wished they all would, but few could assimilate the data and possess the passion to relay this information to a customer who has the desire to know just a little more about this man. Of course I had accumulated vast amounts of information, since discovering him just a short time ago in 1996, but that was to further my personal knowledge. But I should voluntarily share some of this information when requested to do so.

Where could more information be obtained without going back into the archives from some opinionated media interviews or imposing on Kitaro himself? The music disk jackets reveal special graphic communications representing nature and the spheres. Record titles would also play an important part in exploring the meaning of the music he is presenting to us. These were just the rudimentary keys in gathering sufficient data to relay to a customer. Subsequently additional disclosures were obtained from other sources.

Once while visiting the San Francisco area in the spring of 1998 I discovered Kitaro's dynamic Broadway score *Cirque Ingenieux* and listened to it repeatedly that day to absorb its full meaning musically.

On another occasion, while visiting Kyoto, Japan during the cherry blossom season in 1999, I stopped in a music store and found many new albums I had not known about. The department manager and sales lady took their *Time* to print out Kitaro's discography and I purchased six new, to me, albums for my collection.

Then while visiting the Music Capital of the World, Nashville, Tennessee, in the fall of 1999, I found several out-of–production albums for my collection, which gave me more of the background of Kitaro's work.

Spending three weeks in Thailand, in the spring of 2000, yielded another great find, cassettes of various albums (not available in the U.S) which my customers had been requesting. Later that summer, on a revisit, I found the new release *Ancient*. I had not been informed by the record company that it was coming. I purchased two cases from the clerk, who thought I was crazy, three months prior to the U.S. release. My customers were very happy with this find.

Again in 2001, in San Diego, I found more albums in LP which I didn't have; the customers would want these for there collections.

To continue my quest for more of Kitaro's works, patrons often participated by forwarding Kitaro's older works and some provided information from the Internet, and his neighbors in Japan revealed his character. A logo printing company forwarded a case of sweatshirts with Kitaro's picture on the front. Record companies and music distributors made contributions to my quest. This man is beyond the average artist and by no means created and groomed for acceptance by the public, or he is a flash in the pan artist with a musical style whose main purpose is to produce melodies of like style which the general public would be attracted to buy. For Kitaro to produce his music in today's environment, within the *Scope* of obvious world chaos, has to be ignored; one must proceed with what can be done to comfort the *Innocent People*. The general public didn't, doesn't and probably never will realize, what he genuinely represents. All they have to do is just enjoy the effects of the music and receive from it what they are capable of understanding.

For those who have followed Kitaro's work, from his early days, I feel envy. For some of you are aware of the pervading simple theme that encompasses all aspects of his connate awareness that is expressed musically, without words, leaving room for individual interpretations...and most importantly, personal *Scope* and growth.

For those who desire instant gratification, I regret I must report that it cannot be revealed. It has to be experienced. Liken to an explanation of the workings of electricity. Unscrew the light bulb and stick your finger in the socket.

However, listed below is a taste of definitions to a finite sampling of record titles:

The first album, *An Enchanted Evening* begins with track three- titled *Dance of Sarasvati*. Who is Sarasvati? She is the wife of Brahma, the god of all worldly things in the Hindu religion. She is the goddess that invented the perfect written and spoken language of Sanskrit. She is the goddess of intellect, poetry and music. Her origin is in the region of the sacred *Ganga* River in India where even today the dying are bathed in its waters for spiritual preparation for their *Astral Voyage* after the body dies. Kitaro has composed this melody especially for the woman. When this song is aired in Spirit house, most of the women do respond positively by natural dance movements, not realizing exactly what they are hearing. *Dance of Sarasvati* closes with the mantra *Ohm Eim Saraswatyei Swaha*, meaning; *Om* and salutations to that feminine energy which informs all artistic and scholastic endeavors, and which *Eim* (pronounced I'm) is the seed. Sarasvati is seen as having four symbolic arms, two hands holding the musical instrument identified as the vina, one hand holding one hundred and eight prayer beads and one hand holding knowledge. She spans the world of mundane knowledge and spiritual understanding. Those pursuing any artistic or educational endeavor whatsoever will gain greatly from the practice of this mantra. Kitaro closes this song with fifty-four mantras of the one hundred and eight for Sarasvati.

Now that Sarasvati was identified and having only a graphic representation of her, I was compelled to acquire her likeness in statuary form. With some difficulty, I did manage to locate a twenty-four inch brass-casting image a distributor claimed he had but couldn't locate. After a two-hour drive and searching his warehouse and showroom she was located and purchased. On the return trip, and experiencing a tire blowout, without any harm, she is now displayed in The Tourist Shop where she remains today for all to see. Subsequently, many others have now contributed beautiful pictures and icons of Sarasvati for display.

Even though Sarasvati originated in India and businesses are named after her there, her purpose and religious significance is being lost or misinterpreted by the very people who worship her. This is evident from the conversations with visitors from that country. Perhaps it is due to personal material priorities? Sarasvati is an integral part of my continued education for additional spiritual awakening and sharing what I can with others, thanks to Kitaro.

The first track of An *Enchanted Evening* is *Mandala*. The word *Mandala* literally means circle and originates from Hinduism and Buddhism. It is a tantric meditation device. Its purpose is to be a visual aid for concentration and introversive meditation, leading to the attainment of insights and to activation of forces culminating in sidhi supernatural forces. The Mandala is a graphic representation of this process. It is not only theoretical, but also practical as an operational scheme involving a clear plan for realizing the process within oneself. It thus becomes an instrument (yantra). There are many types and varieties of mandalas depending on the nature of the central deity. The most classic pattern of mandalas are of the Dhyani Buddha. This pattern appears in the oldest tantrics. The mandala represents the Palace of Purity, a magical sphere cleansed of spiritual obstacles and impurities. The squarc of the Sacred Palace proper is enclosed in multiple circles of flames, ajar, eight cemeteries (appears only wrathful deities) lotus, and the inner

Spirit House

square (to reach the deity of the mandala). This can all be recognized on the compact disk cover artwork of the album, *Mandala*.

It should be noted the mandala is not a game of entertainment nor should it be taken lightly. It takes years of study and much concentration before even attempting to begin one. It is a very sacred and ancient device. Also mandala types appear all over the world such as the American Indian's sand paintings. Several tantric manuals are devoted to the exposition, for the purpose of visualization of groups of complex mandalas.

Tunhuang (Dunhuang) is an oasis in the province of Kansu, in northwestern China, where famous caves were discovered in 1900, from the 5th century known by the name Mo-Kao-ku. Over 40,000 written Taoist and Confucianist scrolls where excavated along with paintings, ritual implements and one of the oldest ink drawings of a mandala known. It stems from the 9th and 10th centuries.

Kokoro (from the heart), the seventh track on the same album, is a Japanese word of Zen origin and translates into, heart, spirit, consciousness, soul, mind or absolute reality – the mind beyond the distinction mind and master (bussho), self-nature, or true nature.

Spirit of Taiko, the sixth track on the same album, is performed on very large vertical Japanese drums; on such Kitaro reaches an altered state of awareness. Since the covering on these drums is from animal skins, it is believed the animal lives when the drums are played and its spirit is released. Similar to stringed musical instruments such as the violin, that uses animal gut, etc.

There is no forthcoming conclusion in my research. We must all find our own laboratory for acquiring self-knowledge. This laboratory could be closer than you can think?

"Sounds are everything. Words sometimes make problems in the world. But sounds, no problems. Sound makes people feel."
Kitaro

CHAPTER SIX

THE DECISION

In June 1998, after all the research and inspiration, the final decision was reached to promote Kitaro's music exclusively within the store, for the primary benefit of the *Innocent People* visiting from all over the world. The actual decision took several months of examining my mental processes. But the source for the final decision was from the customers. After extensive interviews, they had arrived with the final answer. Stock Kitaro's music for them and stock the entire collection. After all, they were the ones who would be the purchasers either directly or by mail order. They were the ones referring Kitaro to their friends, co-workers, relatives and associates, and buying the messenger's music as gifts. Again, being mindful by staying in the present was a declaration that the people were being served by the best method I could conceive.

The record company was contacted and informed of my interest and intent. They began forwarding advertising placards, brochures and pictures, which were displayed through out the store. First came demonstration music and what was considered by me to be educational material of all Kitaro's great work. Second, music distributors were referred and orders begin being placed. Third, business cards and product labels reflected "Music by Kitaro." Then Kitaro's heavenly music was finally made available and played while an orientation of his accomplishments and goals were given, and the people were pleased.

Knowing this orchestration would have to be *From the Heart*, and presented with the most sincere passion I have ever expressed and with natural enthusiasm, to have any degree of success for the people. Having been presented this opportunity to further promote the *Strength* of Kitaro's music throughout the world, from this one-man operation, an exciting and potentially gratifying experience began. The basic foundation was laid for my plan and it was within me. As Dr. Einstein stated, "Imagination is more important than knowledge."

First, without the direct endorsement from Kitaro or his staff to become a self-appointed messenger, providing the public more information about his music, entails the responsibilities of an agent of proper representation. Second, having worked in fiduciary relationships before, this would be a simple self-assignment due to my honorable intent. And finally, if one must ask permission from a gatekeeper, one has not passed through the gate. How could this scheme begin in the most professional manner possible without ever meeting this man face-to-face and only utilizing secondhand information? The answer again lies in his omnipotent music. It was all there.

Kitaro was performing from his feelings and my commitment to his music would be from my feelings. My ultimate desire was for the listener to open up his or her feelings. Kitaro was blessed with the inspiration to create this music and now it's our music to apply as we wished.

CHAPTER SEVEN

SPIRIT HOUSE: THE MAGICAL MEETING PLACE

The original shop that was fashioned back in 1993 with the right diligence, and at the pleasure of the tourists, had now progressed into a recognizable Spirit House to a number of visitors on their *Sacred Journey*. It was immersed consciously, consistently and persistently, and completely into music of the spheres from the music Kitaro was producing since I discovered him in 1996. His music is now guiding me beyond the limitations of thought to other levels of comprehension, transcending logical contradictions and dualistic modes of thought. That is when I realized, I did not select Kitaro's music; his music selected me and precisely when all the conditions were in alignment. It was a natural progression that I could and should share this with the masses who were traveling along life's *Silk Road,* as they were passing through here and I was placed in this position to do that. It was the music, not words to music that was creating varied personal interpretations for some listeners to reach unknown or unexplored feelings. Which was perfect in every aspect. This place now became a haven for continuing spiritual training, not mechanically or intellectually, but with the right thinking and intuitive ability to practice this acquired knowledge with the right concentration of seeing people, places and things as they really are. Also for knowing what to do and what not to do, from ordinary continued everyday exposures that were opportunities for this practicing student to grow. Also, this environment of accelerated and retarded *Time* and space created countless lifetimes of opportunities for me to acquire the right view in observing humanity in its nature state and genuinely meet "self" in all the preferences and prejudices, sense gratifications, egos, illusions, attachments, over and under indulgences and most importantly, my very own self-delusions and ignorances of the world in which I live. Was Spirit House desecrated by Kitaro's spirit?

It has been said since *Ancient* times that the written word is mightier than the sword. But haven't we overlooked the absolute power of music from responsible musicians that has the ability to heal the wounded or bring about our own inner spirituality, or change a certain King's attitude from a would-be executioner to applying mercy when a court musician changed his tune?

Unfortunately, I have witnessed comparative few who would consider trusting music seriously as a tool toward finding lasting peace, changing one's attitude, or, for some degree of enlightenment, be embraced for personal development. Just for spasmodic entertainment or a temporary escape from self-imposed stress. There are those dramatic exceptions such as the lady who asked the funeral director to change the music to a Kitaro CD. She had brought the CD with her to her grandfather's funeral because that's the music he loved in life. Another came to Spirit House and remarked, "I feel something in here." Her young husband had just passed on three weeks earlier from cancer and felt Kitaro's music would help her through this period of loss. She selected *Best Of Kitaro Volume I;* subsequently the production of this album rated as, "...the best seller year after year," was discontinued two months later.

Already having previous knowledge and memorized scores of albums and several hundred record racks of Kitaro's music, a special effort was given to select albums and tracks of music for individuals or groups with a specific interest in mind. Education administrators and nuns made selections for their staff and teachers picked out music for their students for all grade levels. One schoolteacher for special education pupils said, "These children are very receptive to this music." An eighth grade teacher felt Kitaro's music and purchased a compilation album to play for her students and requested additional information on Kitaro himself that she could relay to her students. This music was her first introduction to the messenger. She was given copies of Kitaro's poetry, a Kitaro t-shirt and all the information I had available. Doctors purchased his music for background music for their waiting rooms together with hospital staff including hospice personnel. And an astro physicist purchased Kitaro's music and said, "His music is perfect for the work I do."

Practicing the right mindfulness by staying focused in the moment, with all the constant distractions was a test of my equanimity, and initially a struggle at first. Leastwise, until I realized this was my greatest opportunity to observe my reactions and readiness to an extraordinary *Caravansary* of people to whom I was being subjected. Multiplicities of situations were being presented specifically for my lessons or their lessons and were all becoming clear one by one. The recognition of opportunities in such a high traffic tourist area, without being crushed by the weight of the world's thoughts, created the right action in exposing me to these remarkable events for the mutual benefit of the world for making contact with me and me with them. I became so absorbed in observing and contacting these manifestations of thousands of fluttering butterflies that I now was becoming more aware of the many reflections of the real and false me.

Literally a throng of souls remarked or recorded they had sensed the essence of the store was a "sanctuary", "magical", "peaceful", "heaven" or "touched by the angels". Or they would make remarks, "I was drawn here". There were numerous profound comments directed to me from their hearts that I could only respond by simply saying "thank you". Such as, "I feel I've always known you," "I love you", "God sent me to you," "You are a Gypsy Buddhist," "What a blessing", and "You have made our vacation." Still others said, "I was mysterious, secretive or the chosen one." And still another said, "I don't know why, but I have always wondered why you were here. I didn't feel you belonged here." In any event, perhaps they took a piece of *An Enchanted Evening* with them after signing the guest book and left to the *Dance of Sarasvati*.

What is being experienced now is exactly what was initially projected that I was subjected to four years ago in the tourist shop, when I realized Kitaro's music was having an emotional effect on the people; I would be dealing with human psychology, and without a license. In actuality, with the combination of Kitaro's music, I was deep in the spiritual realm with whomever I was in contact with beyond the reach of scientific measurement that can only be realized with our mind. A subject of great importance to me.

From the very beginning, there was a basic human exchange of spontaneous sharing of personal triumphs and tragedies of life's experiences and expectations and a special spirituality was being enhanced naturally as more contacts were made beyond what could have ever occurred within a typical so called working environment. Such as witnessing customers faint, weep, request the human touch of a simple embrace of love and revelations of their most intimate secrets. At times, these interactions became so intense I would be propositioned to have a meaningful relationship for an hour with them and I felt like an eighteen girl trying to protect her virginity. Scores upon scores of total strangers seemed to seek me out and would make a plea of "Help me… I know you can," "Make me feel good," "I am suffering so much." One example was the Baptist minister who would stop in occasionally asking for my help, who served in the Gulf War as a USA LTC Chaplin, now working at the VA hospital attempting help put lives back together from the Vietnam era. And my long time friend, who was one of the helicopter pilots for the Shaw of Iran, who was now reduced to a taxi driver to support his disabled son and family. This progression lead to an additional understanding of what was being observed and experienced with others but was actually "self". Whether it was good, bad or ugly or would eventually lead to recognizing what to do or what not to do, or stop making similar errors. Fulfilling sense gratifications through people, places and things had almost always lead to disappointment when they didn't last or they didn't continue to meet my expectations. One should always be in pursuit of recognizing things for exactly what they are.

Material gain was not in the formula, but it appeared I had placed myself in the right livelihood to earn a living because financial obligations were always being provided. Realizing that doing your duty, without complaint, sustains happiness. Happiness is the by-product of what we are doing right. Becoming a better or worse person for this effort in actuality is neither, but realizing the duality and being indifferent and not attached to the outcome of situations will bring about less suffering.

I suspect as higher degrees of enlightenment are acknowledged, practiced and applied, personal acceptance by others will diminish until self-realization is reached. In that you are different. You are on the way and alone to exercise this newfound freedom of being unattached; possibly unattachable, and finally become responsible for your own actions. Then choices become obvious. Do nothing but murmur prayers in isolation in a non-active state of prostituting to selfish ends, while humanity is dying in ignorance, or recognize the availability of raw materials, the right speech, available tools in front of you and the *Time* that can be applied and shared with others constructively *From the Heart*.

Other phenomena that should be addressed is what appears to be the safe zone or sanctuary atmosphere emanating from within, around and through Spirit House, which apparently followed me from the old business location. Awareness of this lessened my concerns of the likelihood of ever being directly affected by the evils, chaos, catastrophes and crisis that was occurring all around me in the immediate area. The second phenomenon was realizing that scores of people were returning to me for some degree of restitution, whose initial intention was inconsiderate or had inflicted a monetary loss. Of course there are always those holdouts with a perpetual "war going on inside". One of resentment, envy and hate, drinking their poison and waiting for me to die. However my thoughts and actions were generally exercising my right to see no evil, hear no evil and speak no evil regardless of these events, to the best of my ability.

Due to this unique position of not being isolated or insulated from the real world, the surroundings yielded an undistorted cross section of the run of human beings. One may not desire to break bread with them, or sleep with them, or pray to their god, but they are human beings doing the absolute best they can with that which they have to work. They may be of different color, culture or from another country, but they happen to be on the same planet sharing the identical resources we all are sharing.

Individually they came to Spirit House, representing the patron, looker, solicitor, saint and the nun. Also the prostitute, sinner, con, thief and the liar made their appearance along with those who function within the entrenched bureaucracies with their self-serving agendas. Those who are not practically protecting and serving their employers and treat the human as a commodity for their profit center. A *Mirage* of thousands upon thousands came with their own degree of suffering and it appeared no one escaped. Spirit House and the messenger have been exposed to them all, comparable to a continuous filmstrip of an old movie. A few identified so closely with the human animal they would be tribal in nature by adorning their bodies with metal rings, hooks and other whirligig things protruding from their body parts, strange things. For everyone to see, including permanent painted figures on their skin. Others were obviously in the early stages of training to become an old person of poor physical, mental and spiritual health. Some, such as the beggars, street people and homeless have written their own job descriptions to leave the mainstream and forge out their own survival, basing their future existence on past experiences. And that is okay. Others are proud of their high corporate positions, accumulated material wealth but would give it all away if their daughter would give up drugs and come home. Those of pure love are the caregivers, hospice workers, nurses, doctors and others working under adverse conditions. Regardless of who or what they appear to be or what their function is, they're human beings with the potential of becoming better persons than they are at the present. Our patience and compassion should be shown to them and ourselves.

Another group almost forgotten about, in our unique culture, are the dying elderly parents who gave their *Agreement* to give the best there was, to give their children who have now abandoned them in emptiness and despair, mentally and physically and financially harmed, helpless and hopeless and some accused of bad parenting by their adult children, for whatever justified reasons; finally they are warehoused with others of their kind while they wait to enter the gateless gate abused and confused about their imminent journey they're about to take.

It appears the whole cycle begins again with some of our missing children by stripping them of their immortality and innocence of their little minds, or abusing their little bodies, as the other human animals gather around to form and shape their future (from their learned biased points of view or leave them with no guideposts to experience the *Winds Of Youth* to fend for themselves leaving society responsible for their actions, in the end).

Now, with *A Passage of Life,* I have come full circle and all my efforts, at this stage, are only a check of my own progression. I thought I had begun this effort for a self-serving purpose, only to make the transition to share with those who did not know; to reap the benefits for my self-knowledge, by allowing everyone to become a winner, thanks to Spirit House. At times, I wonder what my next earthly adventure-lesson will be, for I realize and completely understand that Spirit House, and its function, will dissolve and disappear, as I will, when this phase of *Time* is completed as it should be. In my reality, I didn't begin it, nor will I be responsible for ending it. For neither beginning, middle nor ending exists, only my perception of it. Kitaro's song titled *Nageki* translates to be grieved and regret. I would grieve this passing, but I would not regret what transpired in Spirit House. I now await the next crescendo or "Gurdjieff" shock for change and more self-knowledge.

"I like to follow more natural movements. All of my songs come from nature. I express nature by my music."
Kitaro

CHAPTER EIGHT

RESPONSE

I had always assumed the majority of these people were hearing Kitaro's music but were not listening. This proved to be the case when 95% of all purchases were made by this first time exposure to Kitaro. Many of these first time buyers responded with surprise such as, "Where have I been." "I didn't know he did the music for that..." "These are all of his albums?" At times, I felt like I was responsible for the music when I was only the self-appointed messenger of Kitaro and his music. Many more revelations were to unfold for my education into this realm of *Kitaro's World of Music* and *The World of Kitaro*.

For a period, at each point of purchase of a Kitaro album, every customer was given a brochure of his work and as a special thank you gift of a miniature angel that one lady called, "Little ambassadors for the world." It was not important if these people purchased the messenger's music or not. What was most important was that they were exposed to it, they listened to it and that they felt it? The majority for the first time and it moved their spirit. Some previous Kitaro customers would call me and request an album to be mailed and, on occasion, would request I play the album while holding the phone to the music so they could make a decision. Some were buried so deeply with financial obligations leaving them with no discretionary funds even for the price of an album that had the potential to lift their soul. Others claimed they would be back to purchase an album, and many many did. It was amazing that some would leave only to return moments later to buy a CD. I would sense in others that they would probably buy an album later from the Internet to save a few bucks?

As the new technology came along, a man told me, "I'll download it from the Internet and cut my own CD," without as much as a thank you for introducing him to Kitaro. My response was, "At least you came out a winner." An epilogue to this story is that this man humbly returned a month later and asked for my help in selecting two albums for his wife's birthday. Subsequently this man's wife returned for two more albums and donated currency from their country for display. This was truly an experience from Russia with Love. Whatever their decision, I did my duty and I attempted to always express some degree of equanimity. (It should be noted that many musicians are lucky if they net $1 for each CD sold. For every CD sold, many are copied illegally killing the music industry.)

It seemed the whole spectrum of humanity passed through Spirit House listening to my orientation of this great artisan. Some were numb, or so-called unconscious, to the music they were hearing; some skeptical of my orientation, or it was just the presentation of an old sales pitch or glorification of an ordinary musician; yet others appeared as ghosts without any purpose whatsoever. Again and again, I presented each of them the best I had to give and the rewards could not be measured.

One mother said, "While I was expecting, I would play Kitaro's music and when our baby was born and when we couldn't stop her from crying we would play his music. That was the only thing that worked." Another couple purchased an album for their wedding background music. And an expectant mother, in two days, wanted a Kitaro album for her new born baby and later ordered more. I informed a Kitaro fan of one of his new releases and asked if I could demonstrate it and she said "No! I trust him, I'll just buy it."

Approached by someone with a particular desire to relax, reduce stress or find peace is when I felt I could excel by going to the right album and track, matching the music with the customer's needs after gathering precise information from them or feeling their true concerns. No music store would give them this kind of attention. My passion was paying off. I could now apply what I was learning and helping the people, even as a lay person. Many of these people were so grateful for some degree of help or just being introduced to Kitaro that they would request a hug from me; some would follow-up with simple "thank you" calls and notes and many would offer their change from the sale as my tip.

Some customers have emphasized to me that Kitaro's music is "only synthesized" or electronic, in the context that it is not real music? I would wonder how far their lives had become synthesized? My friend Mr. Webster states, "Synthesized is the putting together of parts or elements to form a whole." I would often wonder how far their lives have become synthesized? Little do they know Kitaro is self-taught on scores of other musical instruments including many *Ancient* instruments, he has collected from around the world that he plays with passion on stage.

Then on Mother's Day 1999, it was arranged for me to meet Kitaro backstage. He had just given a grand performance to a meager audience in a small farming community in California. This was my second Kitaro concert attendance since attending his live performance in December 1997, at the California Center for the Arts. This meeting was almost three years after being introduced to his music and less than one year after committing Spirit House to his music for the people.

I initially greeted Kitaro in his language and with the proper feelings and gestures. I continued to inform him that I had dedicated his music exclusively to my small shop at the request of the many visitors. I also acknowledged that my only desire was to contribute to getting his message out to the world. Pictures were taken together and later displayed throughout Spirit House.

I was so proud of meeting Kitaro that I mailed my mother a framed picture of Kitaro and myself. She hung this picture in her home with pride but later said she had taken our picture down and put it in the closet. At first, I couldn't understand why she did this until she revealed her reasoning. She told me, "The little guy in the picture (Kitaro) disappears at times and reappears. Sometimes I have a man standing, who appears behind me with a scarf over his head." To this day, she refuses to re-hang this picture out of fear of seeing something she doesn't understand. Another lady, from Rio, Brazil, had similar remarks when she watched a live Kitaro concert there at the Metropolitan Theatre. She said, " You know he (Kitaro) doesn't have a body." I told her, "We'll not talk about it at this time." She purchased a Kitaro CD and left the store. Many other similar comments were made to me, from Kitaro patrons, along these lines over the years.

As of this writing, over twenty thousand hours of Kitaro's air has been consciously vibrated in this *Oasis* and many thousands of albums have been purchased from Spirit House instilled with love and affection since discovering him and promoting his music from *Heaven and Earth*. From that point on, one album begot two and two albums begot four and four albums begot eight and so on, as these patrons returned to their realms around this world and acquired more albums. By word of mouth others were enlightened, who enlightened still others for their peace and healing through the magic of Kitaro's wordless music. Some remarked that I was "obsessed" or a "fanatic" with Kitaro's music and I would reply, "Thank you for that information. Shouldn't everyone be?" They did not know this was the path I had chosen… for them. Some people would perceive sound, look at Kitaro's pictures and comment, "You must be a real Kitaro fan?" Not even taking a moment to realize who he is or what they were hearing and left the gold behind. This became another lesson for me. How many times upon countless times had I been exposed to gold and didn't recognize the opportunities when the Universe flashed it before my senses?

Knowing human nature, I could only speculate that some would think I was becoming a neurotic with Kitaro's music or I hero-worshiped him or I was being overindulgent with the music and becoming dependent. These analyzes could only come from the uninitiated who have missed the entire point.

Due to a degree of success I was experiencing with Kitaro's music, I was told by a music company executive, "I wish I had a thousand guys out there like you." Implying his only concerns were sales. Not the healing power of Kitaro's wordless music that has given so many but just focusing on using the power of music to make money? Not being directly involved with the music industry, I have found there exists extreme competition between recording artists, record companies and distributors. At one point, I discovered that Kitaro's complete line of discography had been deleted from a major sister wholesale music distributor's spring/summer 2000 catalog. A mistake? Also, in their subsequent issues, they too only made available a small fragment of his work. I had also discovered the chief contributors of Kitaro's music group were abandoning the ship. Why? A few of Kitaro's award winning albums were discontinued or reshuffled among vapor corporations. Why? I kept my front lines supplied with Kitaro's music as they rearranged the deck chairs on their Titanic. The bottom line was that I committed to supplying these patrons with Kitaro's music so long as he produced his heavenly music. I had to report to a much higher source. About this, I did become obsessive.

I found some artists are being marketed regardless of quality that the average unsuspecting consumer buys and later finds the content unsatisfactory, or experiences diminishing returns, or is detrimental to them or society. The used music section in music stores is filled with it, except for Kitaro and a few other responsible artists who have withstood the test of *Time*.

Along the way, I met an x-roadie for Pink Floyd, who purchased a Kitaro album, and shared additional insight into the musician's struggles. A "golden opportunity" presented itself. An executive from a film company that produced one of the films Kitaro was awarded (Soong Sisters) for the music soundtrack remarked, "I felt I was supposed to be here (Spirit House). He later delivered a copy of that movie as a gift to me. Also a V.P. of a major music distributor was astounded Spirit House was dedicated to Kitaro's music. I informed him of the customer's needs and wants and he forwarded promotional material on Kitaro's music so I could give it to the customers. Another remarkable event is about a mother who was given Kitaro's *Peace On Earth* album, by a friend, who had bought it in

Spirit House a few weeks earlier. She discovered her daughter's picture in the album insert with the International Peace Choir. She came in to meet with me and express her feelings of elation and remarked, "We were supposed to come in here today. . .thanks for the synchronicity!"

Obviously we are in the presence of a meeting place of messengers who gather for a purpose beyond the limitations of conventional or tangible human understanding, or scientific measurement, for the purpose of, "There is no beginning and there is no end," to self-knowledge.

Along the way, music distributors would forward scores of demos created by other artists they were promoting for my review and consideration, but the majority of them didn't compare to the spirit, soul shaking and shock of Kitaro's vibrations. My patrons agreed. It seemed everyone wanted to jump on the bandwagon and march to the drumbeat of the *Spirit of Taiko*. Some other shop owners suggested other music or would bring samples of what they considered comparable artists to try. Again, there was little substance behind their music. Some of it was little more than pretty music or a fad artist that could not possibly endure the test of time as Kitaro has. Even with his specialized audience. A young and upcoming piano player with potential and a Native American Indian gave me copies of their best work for the store. I wish them the best.

Being pulled this way or pushed that way, to blend in other music artists, became my reality check, which was a healthy consideration. Perhaps only playing Kitaro's music in the store was being obsessive? Or maybe I was going off the deep end? But having the direct feedback from the customers and the benefits they were receiving was enough evidence that the store was, is, and will continue to be on the right track. Otherwise Spirit House would become nothing more than a "wherehouse" for all music and the majority of Kitaro's music would again sink into an Atlantis, becoming a buried treasure. We all need these special artisans of this world to help relinquish some of the sadness and self-imposed sufferings of the human condition.

What became really astonishing, from direct customer feedback, over ninety-five percent of all purchases of Kitaro are from those who claim they have never heard of him. It is beyond the S*cope* of this writing to detail this monopolized situation and why it is occurring. But in brief, my research revealed why many upcoming artists never get published and why many quality artists never get distributed properly, due corporate greed and manipulation up and down the music chain, depriving the consumer of his potential mental joys. I also discovered the identical monopolized situation, by a handful of vapor corporations, has been occurring for centuries with literature that has the potential to lift the human spirit to new levels but is so deeply buried, banned or burned. Kitaro has only sharpened his musical skills over the years. But another unqualified consideration could be that the messenger should not be a mainstream artist and that no single music category could possibly cover the variety, flavors, depth, and spiritual healing of his work. Broadway scores and movie soundtracks that cover the signature of Kitaro's music is real music that expresses it all.

On the other hand, some old Kitaro fans have retained his early works but did not followed his career. Why? From debriefing many earlier Kitaro fans from the seventies, I discovered in general, they never stayed with Kitaro's development, but explored other musical areas through the years. It seems those x-fans got lost into the work of other artists who were popular at the time, and drifted away from Kitaro's original attraction of developing a higher part of their mind and became overwhelmed or entrapped with the material struggle. Now I see a small percentage, of some old Kitaro fans, come full circle and return after being given a personal orientation and update of his work that no music store could do.

Frequently customers would make typical comments such as, "I felt drawn into this store." "I don't know why, but I had to come in." "Music is the essence of life and it is here." Kitaro's music should be the background music for life." "I feel the presence of God in here." "This music goes with the store." "It is peaceful here." " I feel that I want to stay in here." "This store is like a sanctuary." "This music is a breath of fresh air." "This music shakes my soul." Their correspondence through letters and thank you notes are just as revealing, "Kitaro still makes me cry." "Brilliant." "Love Kitaro." "Continue to deliver the message." "Thanks for the memories in a magical shop touched by the angels." And they would telephone to express, "Thanks for being introduced to Kitaro." "I can't believe his music." "The music opens the doors to my heart and soul to paradise or Heaven." "Please forward another Kitaro album." or "You should work for Kitaro." And I would reply, "I am working with him." Many repeat customers would return, year after year, for more music demonstrations and make selections for themselves or for gifts. What a blessing.

As stated previously, *Kitaro's World of Music* is not for everyone or everyone is not ready for *The World of Kitaro*. To be genuinely appreciated for its beauty and mental joys, *The World of Kitaro* must be discovered precisely at the right *Time* as I have discovered it.

A most direct confirmation that the messenger's music has a most penetrating consequence to the soul, came from a lady who commented, " I can't take this music…I can't believe how intrusive and personal it is." Another said, "I love Kitaro's music but my husband won't let me play it in the house." "I couldn't buy this type of music, it's too relaxing." Or another lady stated, " It's spooky in here." My reply was, "It's more spooky out there (implying outside Spirit House)." And another commented, "This sounds like Halloween music (from: *Dream/Mysterious Island)*…it's scary." And then he left. It should be mentioned that a minority of customers did remark they couldn't buy Kitaro's music because they had labeled him a Buddhist or something other than their own religious label. What a pity to be self-deprived of this musical joy. But another was so moved by the album *Peace On Earth* (Christmas) and became compelled to buy it and left muttering, "But I am a Jew. But I am a…" The only comfort I could tell her, it's all right, enjoy the music.

One lady made a dramatic statement that warrants consideration after the tragedy of the World Trade Towers saying, "We should direct Kitaro's music to those who were responsible in an attempt to tame them." If one recalls from history, the reciprocal method utilizing music and the spoken word was broadcast for the demoralization of the advancing enemy (Americans) by Tokyo Rose and Axis Sally. As one researcher stated, 'One who works with sound is therefore manipulating the source of all we touch and see, taste and smell." Somehow I had even realized that fact when making the decision to sell Kitaro's music in the store.

As the years passed, along the way, two additional responsible artists (Frank Steiner I-Ching in 1999 and Karunesh Zen Breakfast in 2001) were discovered and blended in; they became a compliment to Kitaro's music. My patrons agree. This small transition to search out special artists has become a natural progression after my intense exposure to *The World Of Kitaro*, to the third degree of musical inspiration.

Simply stated, all these responses validate the positive impact of Kitaro's wordless spiritually penetrating music from *Heaven And Earth*, regardless.

"My basic idea: new creations by traditional peoples."
Kitaro

"My ultimate goal is to keep expressing my feelings in music and for people to enjoy it."
Kitaro

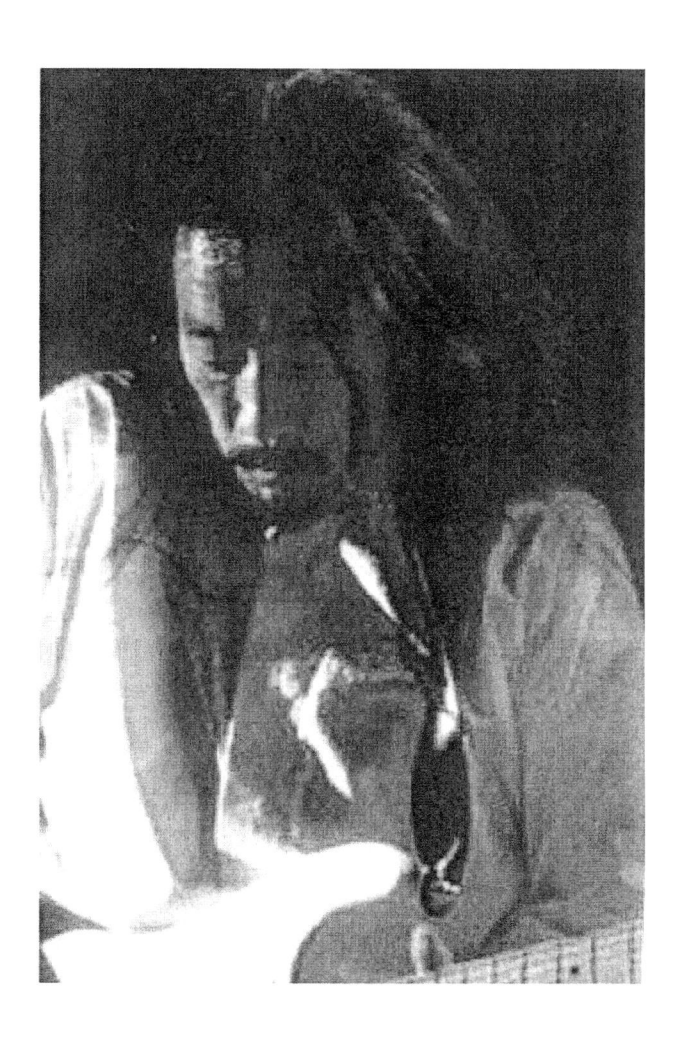

CHAPTER NINE

PASSION, PULP AND PROFITS

Without seeing darkness one could not realize the *Light of the Spirit*.

As passions are pursued, in earnest, weeding through pulp literature, music, seminars and clubs, that claim Divine revelations or promise enlightenment, become a major concern there exists irresponsibility in all today's arts, sciences, music, philosophers, politics, business, etc. that were generated solely for the purpose of personal, bureaucratic or corporate profit. Perhaps many of these have forgotten the basics or never realized, that is, with these acquired freedoms responsibility follows.

Once a passion is surrendered, rightness will show you the way, but be prepared to recognize the opportunities, proper materials, people and thinking that will be offered. For example, most literature available on the *Ancient* practice of Feng Shui concerns the living, working and business conduct through the proper use of the earth's energy lines. This practice takes years of dedicated study and thousands of dollars to implement into an environment to have any degree of success. But just for the cost of a book on the subject, one can become an instant expert in an evening and further education can be obtained though workshops introducing buzz words and phrases to impress their friends and potential clients for the purpose of fulfilling the needs and wants of both parties. Many succumb to a study of philosophy or a religion that has been presented from a foundation of partial truths that fit their perceptions and is fresh, painless and comfortable, not realizing it is not the whole truth or a twisted truth they are hiding behind. Bookstores are filled with this pulp and again for the purpose of fulfilling the needs and wants of both parties. But the truth is primary even when one's piers, associates and friends are in disagreement. At times, one will even question oneself.

I have found, on occasion, some professional writers get caught up in the frenzy and lure of writing, for the reward of money and fame, leaving the reader with no real substance or creativity for pursuing their enthusiasm; however a pretty and hyped-book cover jacket and numerous counter endorsements, by other professionals they have quoted and quoted again in subsequent books, and by other authors of bibliographies of works cited are their reward.

As my passion has matured into a desire of awakening even more people to the personal benefits of Kitaro's music, I find myself exploring alternatives beyond the confines of Spirit House, but on the fringes of a fatal personal error. Researches lead to a generally misused, impersonal and prostitutor tool-system, commonly known as www/computer. This machine and its operators appear to function insensitively to any customers needs and wants by conducting commerce behind cold computer screens selling and buying by eliminating the ultimate fear-of-face to face contact. Much like a predator and his weak victim having an encounter in total darkness. The full time hunter will win the game. Similar to how hellevision has evolved today with gross information of misinformation. Leading the victim into its trap. It appears when truth and justice for everyone is abandoned and when the primary concerns shift from helping others, to an attitude of what I can get out of it, personal and corporate doom and financial collapse will follow.

What was discovered on www/computer is that everyone, music specialists and the general stores, have jumped onto the bandwagon and presented their half-baked version of a very small and fragmented collection of Kitaro's work. Where were they twenty-five years ago when he (Kitaro) probably needed them? Much of this meager product presentation is mislabeled; some is grossly overpriced, back ordered, two-week delivery times and focused only on instant profits. But again these soon to be vapor corporations are fulfilling the partial needs of both parties.

A few dedicated fans and followers have created their own websites in honor of Kitaro to share information, discography or create a Kitaro fan club of sorts. But most have misinformation or more questions than answers.

As for me, back here in this one-man operation, I continue to give my very best presentation of Kitaro to potential customers, that of a warm orientation of his noteworthy accomplishments while guarding my knowledge of his private life and allowing the customers to buy what fits their needs. Am I the fool? I think not. To date, I have had a full and rich life of experiences privileged only to a chosen few. To see the smiles, receive the thanks and human exchange of feeling on a person to person, on the front lines of life, is more rewarding than hiding behind a computer screen.

For now, in the final analysis, I have no competition and why would I wish to compete with those who have no substance? Also, I am not enthralled with any entity while presenting Kitaro to the world that has been drawn to my door. I am the one offering Kitaro's entire collection in all the available formats and titles. The www/computer groups are depriving his followers and newcomers of this due to selective sales for maximum profit and making decisions what the public wants and deserves from Kitaro and other responsible artisans. But from my experience, the public will discover Kitaro's original ethereal music when their *Time* is ripe as other dead musicians are decomposing.

Also the www/computer is filled with misinformation, mystery, disjointed Kitaro forums, non-responsive Kitaro fan clubs, starving fans with a thirst for more information about Kitaro and his available albums and there are numerous requests for public performance itineraries. As a novice marketer, with information and product to the above needs, I could not possibly fill those needs single-handedly so I came to the understanding that a man must know his limitations. I would have entrapped myself into PASSION, PULP AND PROFITS and could have misplaced my very own inner peace and most assuredly misplaced any gains of self-knowledge. By counting my blessings to have been in a position to touch so many spirits personally, should be recognized as my highest reward for the right livelihood. For this is my fast-forward to a higher degree of enlightenment.

However, Kitaro's many worldwide fans, enthusiasts, and newcomers created Spirit House and this Magical Meeting Place. They were the messengers that frequented my store and initially made their request to carry his music. They had now purchased thousands of his albums and videos, and continued to make their appeal that his complete works should be supplied to a wider worldwide audience due to the fragmented supplies that typically exists in the retail marketplace, leaving the fan or follower to fend for themselves for the *Scope* of Kitaro's work.

Was I ignoring all of them again, as I did with their first request, and now with their second request in creating a Web site, due to my own fears and ignorance? Or was I frightened I might loose my "one on one" relationship while personally presenting Kitaro's work to mostly new people for their first time and experiencing their energy? I felt I had done so much for so many for so little; perhaps, I needed to re-evaluate my decision for my own worldly survival. As stated before, there was a downside if I continued to follow my feelings just to earn a living, giving my all to the people, would leave me behind without a future retirement or dental plan and no gold watch at the end. I would be working without a safety net like performing on a *Solar Trapeze,* as in *Cirque Ingenieux.* Perhaps this was my next path to follow. I had learned how to harness my passions, weed through the pulp, and make profit from the right livelihood. I thought I knew it all and had been on the right track, and I was and discovered I knew nothing. Perfect!

Exactly at this point of revising this chapter, in the late evening of 22 March 2002, within moments customers begin flocking into my store and purchased these auspicious album titles; 2-*Ancient* CD's, 2-*An Ancient Journey* CD's, 1-*Light of the Spirit* CD, 1-*Thinking of You* CD and 1-*Zen Breakfast* CD! The purchasers were the two typical spiritual ladies that occasionally make their appearance to me when I needed them. I didn't know it, as they have done over the years, only with different names and faces, a man of Japanese descent and a man of Middle Eastern descent. As human beings, how many Universal flash cards do we have to be shown to get the picture for what we should do and what we should not do? How much clearer does it have to become for we, as hosts on this planet, we call home, and coming as guests from outside creation? The energy was everywhere. Unbelievable! I just sat in shock and amazement of how far I had come since beginning my little tourist store back in September 1993. I had come and gone beyond beyond and recognized the Messenger?

My final decision to create an exclusive Web site, dedicated to Kitaro's music for those *Innocent People,* came in November 2001. Subsequently, Kitaro's major record company was very supportive and contributed to this effort by supplying the data and graphics required for a professional Web site design named www.kitaroconnection.com. However, there were those "other" Kitaro record distributing/publishing companies that resisted contact with me. I knew, in time, I would also gain their support because, once they realized my motivating passion and their greed to increase overall sales, it would be a marriage made in *Heaven & Earth.* Combined with my years of Kitaro research and experiences, I was directed every step of the way to proceed into the unknown realm of cyberspace and e-commerce. Ready or not, I was doing it my way. Why did it take me so long to come to this decision in such a short period of time?

Passions to attain self-knowledge for realization of who, what, where, when, how and why should not be dependent upon pretty music, pulp books, clubs, seminars, faiths, religions, gurus, individualities or nature gods; you must possess the confidence to seek out your own path, going to the sole source: you and only you. Although credible media, verbal knowledge and divine intervention is available when it is ready to be received. So it has been written "so shall it be done", when the student is ready the messengers will appear.

"I feel this is my mission, connecting the people, connecting the spirits of all over the world beyond nations."
Kitaro

CHAPTER TEN

THE JOURNEY-
A RECAPITULATION INTEGRATING:
The "JAPANESE CONNECTION."

My journey began with my birth in America during an era of war with Japan. This was my earliest glimpse of "the little people" and what they were utilizing we discarded. How coincidences and synchronicities of other personal Japanese encounters along life's path, allowed me to witness dramatic economic shifts in both countries. In the interim, experiencing the darker side when I found myself was sleeping with an adversary; being a guest and accommodated by top Japanese corporate executives, and how my journey continues today working with the music produced by one of the most elite musician's magicians from Japan.

PERSONAL BACKGROUND

During my early teen years, I had my first Japanese encounter while cutting trees down for the local saw mill. One day I saw a group of little people off in the distance of the forest and asked who they were (*Mori no Tami*)? They were from Japan and had purchased the stumps of those trees that had been sawn down. They would grub out these stumps taking them back to Japan to be made into beautiful woodcarvings with natural wood grain swirls and twists for all sorts of decorative and functional items.

WORK ENVIRONMENTS

Early on, my father and I were employed at a company at the

same *Time*. He was working as a machinist and I was working in the Polaris Missile arming and fusing device program, in a secret area with several engineers. At times, I would leave my secured area and go down into the bowels of the machining area and take a break with my father. On one occasion, my father looked up to the catwalk leading from the restricted area where I worked and said, "Look at that." "What?" I said, He said, "Look at that Jap." I then informed him that was my electronic engineer friend Toki with whom I worked. My father made a scowling face and then finished his coffee. Obviously he was still suffering from the combat he encountered 16 years after the war, proving that "We are what we are from where we came from when." Unless we elect to change by digesting the past, and move on, we will bring about our own sufferings year after year.

At the age of twenty-four, in 1967, I was married in Phoenix Arizona and we had moved back to Indiana for the purpose of finding employment. I was about to witness a significant piece of industrial history, the beginning of the collapse of the U. S. steel industry that would have an effect on thousands of Americans. I had managed to secure a job at Ingersol Steel, cold rolling ten-ton coils of stainless steel. One day I noticed an entourage of visiting Japanese businessmen in hard hats, taking notes while touring our facility. I ask management what their (Japanese) purpose was in visiting our plant? I was told, in effect, the Japanese wanted to secure dependable and solid sources of supply for their upcoming steel demands and they had suggested certain upgrades in production methods and modernizing of plant equipment. But the old Pittsburgh hard core management couldn't see the steel for the demand of the ore.

History now tells the tragic story of what happened to the American steel industry, the people and the communities in which they lived due to our arrogance and lack of foresight, etc. And the Japanese were forced into producing their own steel to meet Japanese production demands. At that time, I new something wasn't right. Later on, I always wondered why I was a witness to this

Japanese encounter and was privy to insider information? Later I had managed to be employed by state of the art aerospace and ordnance manufacturing industries that provided the specialized education, technical experiences, disciplined environments, salaries, social interactions and most importantly, motivation for further education. Let's not forget the sense of security. But, we were producing death machines with the potentiality of total destruction of the world and justifying this negative effort with politics, religious beliefs and economics at all levels.

JAPANESE MAGNETISM

Over the years, I continued working for these ordnance and aerospace companies with many multi-national administrators and engineers and found those of Japanese origin were hardworking, focused and left little to chance. I could depend on them to be consistent and persistent.

While employed at Motorola Government Electronics Division, in Scottsdale Arizona, we would attend workshops and seminars for "continued education." On one occasion we attended a very informative talk on the reason Motorola, commercial side, lost the Quasar television due to 40% production line rejects and how Panasonic purchased the Quasar line and made a profit their first year and still retained the original American employees!

Motorola had become so complacent and detached from their production employees, et al and wouldn't listen to their suggestions. Not only did the Japanese correct that problem but they gathered firsthand information from the technicians in the field that were repairing those units. Motorola also informed us that we Americans operate as a confrontational society where the Japanese, at that time, operated more in a concessionary environment, where communication between management and employees was more open.

Currently our general corporate attitude has evolved into loyalty to the stockholders first and instant profits. The days of taking care of your employer and he will take care of you and taking care of the employee and he will take of you is gone. RIP, we had Dr. Deming's guidelines and we didn't follow them for the test of time. Now our corporations go on welfare through government multi-million dollar bailout loans, due to their gross mismanagement, sticking the public with the bill, but are reluctant to give a 14 year-old unwed mother $100 a month. Now the Japanese suffer from some of the identical plagues as the Vapor Corporations appear and dissipate as the clouds do above us.

On November 21,1864, President Abraham Lincoln wrote a letter to colonel William F. Elkins. He wrote, "I see in the near future a crisis approaching that unnerves me and causes me to tremble for the safety of my country. As a result of the war, corporations have been enthroned, and an era of corruption in high places will follow, and the money power of the country will endeavor to prolong its reign by working upon the prejudices of the people until all wealth is aggregated in a few hands and the Republic is destroyed. I feel at this moment more anxiety for the safety of my country than ever before, even in the midst of war."

THE WAR INSIDE

Sometime later in life, my father gave me his Japanese battle flag that he had taken from a fallen Japanese soldier, along with his hometown newspaper clipping. At the time, this gift was more precious to me than him. I based those feelings on his failed attempt to be a dad, by not being man enough to keep his family together, from years gone by.

Later in life, I had met a surviving Kamikaze pilot at a Mesa, Arizona air show and a survivor of the Hiroshima bomb, Takashi Hinomura, who said, "I pray thanks to God everyday that I am still here," who went on to become one of the top kimono producers in Japan. Over the years, this man has revisited my store in San Diego frequently. He is a living piece of history from a troubled time period. I also met a retired Japanese banker from

Yokohama who couldn't believe I would admit I was a descendent from a beaten race: the American Cherokee Indian.

My father died in 1983 from cancer, and I continued my war inside for him through 1993, until I woke up. I realized if I had been given the identical environments and conditions of war, he had been given, the outcome may have been the same for me. After experiencing my own marriage break-up, my children cutting–off all communications with me, things became even clearer. That's when I decided to fall back and regroup for 7 years living alone and eventually relocated to Southern California to begin again.

SLEEPING WITH THE ENEMY

Within a year, after moving to California, I met a lady, a Japanese lady, and we eventually purchased a house together as an unmarried couple. The initial attraction was she spoke five fluent languages, graduated from Kieo University, Tokyo, graduated with an MBA degree from Berlin University, Germany and had spent several years living in Europe as a hippie but currently held a high position with a Real Estate developer in San Diego. It appeared I had enrolled myself into another continued education program.

I initially looked at this as my opportunity to learn more about the Japanese culture and further my desire to learn more of their written and spoken language. I was later to learn she would be of no help to me and I would be criticized at every junction for even attempting to learn the language, due to my Indiana background. She told me that, "The Japanese are top of the line…" One evening, her visiting Japanese friend overheard her remarks and told her, "Akiko San, even though you think of yourself as an eagle, you should not always show your claws." Needless to say, she was never invited back to our house again.

She had been born in 1939, and had come from a wealthy family. Her father had been a doctor and spent a lot of his time, during the war, in Russia as a diplomat. As the war progressed, she and her mother moved to the relative safety of northern Japan into a small house with a vegetable garden. She told me, when she and her mother returned to Tokyo, at the close of the war, "You people (Americans) had destroyed my mother's house."

Within a short time period, I realized what a terrible mistake I had made, again. I even hung up the Japanese battle flag my father had given me years ago over our sofa realizing our situation was hopeless regardless how hard I tried to make sense out of it. It was my symbolic protest against her conduct towards me. It remained hanging there for years without any reaction from her. Was this due to the affection I had for the Japanese culture or had I blinded myself, or was this just another lesson on the universal agenda I was to learn? This time I was really being exposed to the dark side of reality by her manipulations and control, financial scheming, mental brutality, entrapments, plagued with her limited social skills and total inconsideration for another human being, and she blended it all with drunkenness. Had my father been right about the "Japanese?" I think not. This was just an individual that had gotten herself twisted along the way. I just happen to be in her path?

FOOTPRINTS THROUGH JAPAN

However, within darkness is the seed for the light. The Yin and Yang of life. Plans were being made to visit her sister and brother-in-law in Tokyo during the Shinto Holiday of 1991-1992. Her brother-in-law was Vice President of Mitsukoshi Department Stores in Japan and he was making plans for our stay to visit the Shrines and Temples of Tokyo, Kyoto, Nara and Niko. I attended a performance at Kabuki Theater, rode the bullet train, and was treated to the best accommodations and food. This was truly my Japanese cultural experience of "Footprints through Japan."

My live-in Japanese sponsor, responsible for this educational vacation, was never a happy camper. She remained drunk most of the time, etc., hated the culture and the people and hurried me through the temples claiming, "That all this stuff is crap."

RETURN TO JAPAN

In December 1995, while still residing in my self-imposed Japanese prison camp planning my escape, I made plans for a solo trip back to Japan to savor the culture and people in peace. I visited the Kansai region, Osaka and it's castle and monuments and Sakai, eventually staying in a Buddhist Temple in the mountains at Koyasan. "This is a sacred place unparalleled in the world. It is an environment filled with spiritual feeling." This is Shingon Buddhist mountain community where there are no Western accommodations, only very old Buddhist temples to reside in, which I did. It is beyond my logic why I was compelled or guided to go there.

Six months after my return from Japan, I escaped from my Japanese prison camp and its brutal commander. I looked at it as my graduation. However, I had left a lot of money on the table but I had escaped with my life and my life had now been reduced to living in a small apartment above a Chinese restaurant. What an ordeal I had put myself through due to my latent insecurities and co-dependencies, thinking that all Japanese were as congenial as these individuals I had worked with in the past and not seeing things for what they were. I was wounded from the clamor of it all but totally detached and moving forward again.

PREREQUISITE FOR DISCOVERY

Little did I know everything to this point was synchronicity and a prerequisite for something much bigger for this "barbaric and ignorant Indiana farm boy."

I had established a small retail shop in southern California, in the heart of a major tourist area, that generates six million people annually *Westbound* from around this *Planet.* Initially it had begun as an escape from high stress employment just to earn a living, attempting to discover some extension of *Peace.* Not realized at the time, this operation was not to find *Peace* for my personal welfare but for the visiting public who in turn brought me more lasting

Peace and happiness.

Was I graced with another important discovery (Japanese Connection) that was selected for me by chance? In the fall of 1996, after being given three cassettes of music by Kitaro, a Japanese artist I had never heard of before? This was exactly at the same point in *Time* the Japanese lady I had previously left, of a predator nature with a war going on inside, initiated a legal confrontation with me. This battle of wrangling with attorneys, paperwork, delays, money and time consumed over one year of what appeared as a total waste of every resource on everyone's part except for the attorneys involved. During that episode, I continued running the business in an efficient manner, cried to everyone, appealed to whomever for sympathy, but most importantly, maintained my sanity and accentuated my *Peace*.

How could this be? The answer would lie in the facts. First, I was the one in the beginning who placed myself in harm's way to become the victim again due to my latent insecurities. Second, I believed I already possessed the internal *Strength* to cope with almost any situation that could possibly arise. Third, Kitaro's music seemed to be from the heavens and it was allowing me to believe there was a force protecting and guiding me every step of my way. Was this my ultimate Japanese Connection for continuing my *Astral Voyage?*

A metamorphosis was occurring within me as quickly as the *Dawn / Rising Sun* of a new day. My attitude was becoming more focused on exactly what to hold onto and what to let go of became crystal clear. I was feeling compelled to share this music with all those I came in contact with in a subtle and subliminal way. While the patrons did their shopping, my hopes were that they might feel a little peace before they went on their way, as I had. I never realized the full impact or potency of this music or that I would experience the accelerated growth of self-knowledge I continue to experience today.

I had also found that the personal benefits of hearing, listening and feeling this breath of life, from his music, facilitated me in being a much happier man and also by improving my four senses, enhanced memory and a steady development of music appreciation, and a quest for the understanding of every thing.

The tourists would ask if I sold this music and I would send them to a music store after I gave them an orientation of my limited knowledge of his music. I purchased my first CD player in 1997, while gathering more of Kitaro's work from Asia and the U.S. and studying both him and his music, while preparing myself to represent him properly in the event I decided comply with the wishes of these patrons to carry his music.

THE MESSENGER AND THE MARATHON

I had now become convinced by an overwhelming cross section of people from around the world, to stock Kitaro's entire collection of music in The Tourist Shop. Any merchant could stock his music, and I wished they all would, but few would possess the passion to collect and assimilate the data and to relay this information onto a customer who has the desire to know just a little more about this man. Of course I had accumulated vast amounts of information, since discovering him just a short time ago in 1996, but that was to further my personal knowledge. But I should voluntarily share some of this information when requested to do so.

Educating myself on Kitaro had become a primary task of a tangible importance to me if the store were to represent him accurately and acceptably and make his complete works available to this audience. Initially his music was aired for personal pleasure and for the ambiance of the store, but now the patrons mandated supplying them with his music and more information about Kitaro the person.

Extensive research was consumed in numerous domestic and foreign retail music stores checking for Kitaro stock availability of new releases, category accessibility, available brochures, pricing and the personnel who could answer typical questions about Kitaro, to obtain a feel for that which the public was being subjected. Generally what was found that only six to twelve albums were being stocked which only represented two to five titles of his work. Most of the domestic personnel in these stores did not really know who he was other than he was labeled "New Age." I found this to be a strange marketing situation for such an impressive and diverse artist. Only a true Kitaro follower, fan or fanatic would know what they were looking for, or even if it existed. Obviously Kitaro is not a mainstream artist for very good reasons. His music is spiritually awakening; seductive and penetrating to the soul, and many people are not ready for that.

The conclusion to stock Kitaro's work was finally reached over the course of many months from this research and from the magical moments of debriefing customers while working directly with thousands of Kitaro's previous fans and followers, and those newly introduced to *"The World of Kitaro"* from my tourist store in Old Town San Diego. It became obvious that a clear and present need exists for the benefit of those fans and for future customers.

(From June 1998 thru December 2001, over 3,500 units of Kitaro's music and videos had been purchased directly or mail ordered from this one-man operation while a continuous marathon of over 20,000 hours of his music was played.)

STEPPING STONES FOR SELF-KNOWLEDGE

I returned to Kyoto, Japan, for the third time, during the cherry blossom *(sakura)* season of April 1999 and revisited the old Buddhist temples to savor my decision and reconfirm my heart was true and to gain more energy for the unknown tasks that lie ahead. I had planned to revisit Koyasan again, and stay a few days, but a strange feeling of loneliness overwhelmed me in Kyoto, and I returned to San Diego and my store to be with the fluttering butterflies ("cho cho") that visited Spirit House.

Upon returning from Japan, I discovered Kitaro would hold a concert here in San Diego. This would be my second attendance. This would also be another affirmation for implementing Kitaro's music by serving the people and me as the tool.

CLOSE ENCOUNTER OF THE THIRD KIND

On Mother's day 1999, it was arranged for me to meet Kitaro backstage. He had just given a grand performance to a meager audience in small farming community in central California. This was my third attendance to one of his concerts since attending his live performance in December 1997, at the California Center for the Arts. This meeting was almost three years after being introduced to his music and less than one year after committing my store to his music for the people.

I initially greeted Kitaro in his language and with the proper feelings and gestures. I continued to inform him I had dedicated his music exclusively at my small shop, at the request of the many visitors, in June 1998. I also acknowledged my only desire was to contribute to getting his message out to the world. Pictures were taken together and later displayed throughout my store. Was this a Japanese connection of the third kind, or what?

RESEARCH AND REVELATIONS

As additional studies were cultivated, from Kitaro's music, data was researched and collected which lead to a spiritual path of which I had never dreamed. When one surrenders and becomes receptive to the present (in the moment), a realization of total peace occurs during what appears to be the most unfavorable conditions. These degrees of enlightenment will be a round trip ticket for riding the *Cosmic Wave* to adventure; our imminent death will be of no more of a concern than lying our tired body down at night and going to sleep.

OFFER THAT CAN'T BE REFUSED

As I evolved with this project, I could now justify creating an independent Kitaro Web site dedicated exclusively as a centralized source for Kitaro's complete thirty year musical collection.

Although Kitaro's record company, in 1996, consolidated the majority of his discography from other sources there still remain many compilations, re-releases and videos not readily available from other record companies. At present, Kitaro's works are commingled with many other artisans within each of these record companies. I am now qualified to untangle, unify, and assemble his work under one umbrella. The intent of this Web site will be to make available all out of print releases, current discography, compilations and videos and future releases in all formats, from all domestic and foreign sources.

In conclusion, the record company, Domo Records, is in agreement with my idea, endorses the concept and is supportive. Domo is a Japanese word meaning "Thank You". Is this the final Japanese Connection after experiencing a lifetime of the good, bad and the ugly? I think not.

It seemed I had come a long way, but it was always within me from the <u>beginning</u>, or was it the <u>end</u>...or continuing succession!

THE SAGA SHIFTS

If you recall, the young musician mentioned early in this book, whom I met back in 1999, as we wished him our best, had now produced a collection of four uniquely wonderful unpublished albums of his wordless musical magic; mysterious and ethereal harmonies that summon mental images flashing fast forward to us into the next scene of drama, or find you lingering in passion and peace, or perhaps dancing in the gardens of paradise. One could become inebriated from his harmonies of *Heaven and Earth*. He had now requested that "I" should be his manager to promote his musical career. Who qualified me for this task? Again I was initially reluctant, as I was with stocking Kitaro's music in my store six years ago or creating e-commerce. Now I was being presented with an opportunity to apply everything I learned to assist this prolific musician. My heart was in alignment to guide him and I agreed to do my best utilizing all my skills and knowledge, enthusiasm, and resources as his instrument, as I am, Kitaro's messenger. Again, it would be for the benefit of the *Innocent People.*

I would take orders from the patrons for his unpublished music, and again, record their comments as I did with Kitaro, gathering information and finding the precise path to share his music with a wider audience. Creating e-commerce seemed to be the direct path avoiding any conventional music publishing companies and commingling his work within any distribution network. Working from a single store front would produce finite results with his music being an "unknown." He would also get lost, as Kitaro did, in "wherehousing" his music and getting misplaced among the currently popular and run of the mill musicians.

I cannot read or write music, nor am I a prisoner of any significant musical knowledge, which fortunately allows me freedom. I could now justify giving my energy to this upcoming musician since my stepping-stone was Kitaro and perhaps this again was my function?

CONTINUING JOURNEY

As Kitaro has revealed to us, "There is no beginning and there is no end."

If it had not been for the manifestation of all those remarkable and unforgettable people, my journey through this existence would not have been as accelerated and comprehensive. Their constant influx answered questions and exposed countless human events that were the equivalent of many lifetimes to me. They revealed unsatisfactory environments, material entrapments, family life, relationships, loves, joys, fears and sufferings, religions and faiths with a fusion of all their cultures and races.

Spiritual stimulation was ever present and mutually shared, at whatever degree of individual interpretation or understanding, and all were present at a given moment in the junction of time and space. The messenger's osmotic music had been the missing link, the final ingredient for building a bridge for awakening the miniature universe within each of us, for discovering our individual purpose. This vibratory aid is the equivalency to a *Mandala* as a visual aid is to meditation. This has the influence of becoming a portal to the real inner spirit that is omnipresent for all receptive patrons.

The energy of the store shifted again to a dramatic increase of Kitaro music sales, to be a major supporter for the financial survivorship of the store, as our Nation entered into an economic downturn early in the *Millennia*. Were Kitaro sales just a by-product of sincerely doing my duty for the right reasons or was there a more powerful force involved? This all coincided with a laissez fair attitude of our local bureaucrats to support the area merchants, and the visiting tourists. This situation further degenerated leaving everyone to fend for themselves. But again I seemed to be protected. Was it for the purpose of sharing peace with all those which whom I came in contact?

A real life example came when I was guided to special knowledge, exactly one year after committing the store to Kitaro's music, which I studied in semi-privacy for over two years. Again I was requested to share this information with others who needed it, and I did. Most don't know where their earthly journey will lead them but learning the road signs along the way will eliminate some of the bumpy detours.

When verbalizing these experiences and acquired knowledge, and application, to others of *Peace* sincerely from the heart (*Kokoro*), I have witnessed resentment, envy or forbidding disclosure with some people. I have found it is sometimes best to just express our other half with good gestures, leaving room for individual interpretations, similar to Kitaro's wordless music. For that reason, some people who know don't talk and those who talk don't know. We should all find our own separate path to peace and bliss now or later, but we will find it precisely when we allow our window of *Time* to open.

When I began writing writing about these factual accounts a few years ago, my initial concern was if I was qualified for the task. I had always remained reluctant to ever seriously consider having it

Spirit House

published. But if I did, for whom and what purpose? The answer was constantly flashed right in front of me for what should be done. The answer was literally laid on the doorstep to Spirit House to trip over *Time* after *Time* through the years, even though I didn't recognize the perfect opportunity. The adjacent business owner was an established and reputable publisher, and author of over 50 books to his credit, with subjects ranging from spiritual stimulation, education and history. One day, by chance, I shared with him the work I had been doing and after his review, he suggested it should be published. He even remarked, "I learned a lot." Now I was in mutual agreement with him to publish this information for the *Innocent People*.

In a previous chapter, "I" had relayed "my" feelings that somehow "I" knew Spirit House and its function would dissolve and disappear when this phase of *Time* was completed, as it should be. Now, "I" was being presented with "my" next earthly adventure-lessons with the magic of synchronicity, and the obvious universal law of retarded or accelerated time to be in alignment with other spirits. The completion of "my" website was being delayed for over ten weeks due to forces "I" had no control over which coincided with the publication of this book. Overlapping with this, Domo records was reviewing the manuscript for approval of the material mentioned about Kitaro. These events all coincided with Kitaro beginning his first U.S. tour in four years, in Los Angeles, when "I" was invited to be their "guest," with a backstage pass to meet Kitaro for our second *Time*. In addition "my" retail space lease was expiring in six weeks and "I" had decided not to exercise "my" five-year option when "my" best friend and supplier, who has guided "me" for the past nine years, offered his retail space three times larger than "I" had. He was initially responsible for introducing the retail items that were blended in at the old Tourist Shop, He again had been summoned to play a very important and supportive role on the universal roster of messengers from *Heaven and Earth*.

Now with *A Passage of Life*, is this my final chapter? I don't

believe it is. Our personal *Astral Voyage* of self-knowledge neither begins nor ends while we recognize the opportunities to bring happiness and *Peace Through Kindness* offering some degree of enlightenment to others. We are neither too late nor early on our *Journey* ("tabiji") to balance our passions and actions. It's what is expected of us, it's our duty, now or later. It's our choice to take the right action. We are the student and we are our own messengers and we are the final teacher and student.
 To be continued... forever.

Thinking Of You

"As long as people feel something from my music and it influences them in a good way, that is all that matters to me."
Kitaro

KITARO'S
COMPLETE DISCOGRAPHY AND VIDEOS LIST

AN ANCIENT JOURNEY
ANCIENT
AN ENCHANTED EVENING
ASHU CHAKAN (Asian Teahouse) (TBD)
ASIA
ASIA TOUR SUPER LIVE
ASIAN CAFE
ASTRAL VOYAGE aka TEN-KAI
BEST ALBUM
BEST COLLECTION
BEST OF GRAMMY AWARD
BEST OF KITARO
BEST of KITARO VOL. 1
BEST of KITARO VOL. 2
BEST 16 HITS, KITARO'S
BEST OF KITARO II, THE
BEST OF KITARO III (TBD)
BEST OF TEN YEARS
CIRQUE INGENIEUX
CLOUD (TBD)
DEEP FOREST (TBD)
DREAM
ENDRESS JOURNEY
ESSENTIAL COLLECTION, THE
ESSENTIAL COLLECTION II, THE
FREEDOM CHANTS... (TBD)
FULL MOON STORY
GAIA-ONBASHIRA
HEAVEN and EARTH
IN SILENT (TBD)
HEALING FOREST
INDIA

IN PERSON DIGITAL
IN SILENT (TBD)
JOURNEY to the HEART
JOURNEY to the HEART II
KAISO (TBD)
KARUNA
KI
KITARO COLLECTION
KITARO SPECIAL
KITARO'S WORLD OF MUSIC
KOJIKI
LADY OF DREAMS
LIGHT OF THE SPIRIT
LIVE IN AMERICA
LIVE IN OSAKA (TBD)
MANDALA
MILLENNIA
MORNING LIGHT (TBD)
MU LAND
MUSIC FOR THE SPIRIT
MUSIC FOR THE SPIRIT Vol, 2
MUSIC FOR THE SPIRIT Vol, 3
MY BEST
NIPPONJIN
NOAH'S ARK
OASIS
PARALLEL WORLD
PEACE ON EARTH
SILK ROAD
SILK ROAD COLLECTION
SILK ROAD VOL. 1
SILK ROAD VOL. 2
SILK ROAD SUITE
SILK ROAD JOURNEY SERIES
-ALL   ROADS LEAD TO ROME

-ACROSS THE KARAKUM DESERT
-ACROSS THE PAMIR
-COLLECTION, DVD
-COLLECTOR'S BOX
-IN SEARCH OF WISDOM
-THE SOGHDIAN MERCHANTS
SILVER CLOUD
SOONG SISTERS, THE
SUPER BEST
TAMAYURA
TEN-JIKU aka INDIA
TEN-KAI
TEN TO CHI (TBD)
TENKU
THINKING OF YOU
TONKO
TOWARD THE WEST
TUKUSEN
TUNHUANG
TWIN BEST
VERTIGO
YAKUSHI-JI
WEST
WORLD OF KITARO, THE

MUSICAL CATEGORIES

For customer convenience, it becomes necessary to group as many of Kitaro's albums as possible, since Kitaro's musical signature has stood the test of time and he has produced scores of albums and videos in many different musical categories beyond "New Age."

Please see the partial category of listings below: for a complete description, see Discography and Video Descriptions and Ordering on www.kitaroconnection.com.

Healing and Mediation:
ASIA
ASIA SUPER TOUR LIVE
ASTRAL VOYAGE
ENDRESS JOURNEY
FULL MOON (TBD)
HEALING FOREST
INDIA
JOURNEY TO THE HEART
JOURNEY TO THE HEART II
NOAH'S ARK
SILVER CLOUD
TENJIKU
TOWARD THE WEST
TUNHUANG

Original Movie Soundtracks:
HEAVEN AND EARTH
MILLENNIA, QUEEN
SOONG SISTERS, THE

Classical and Art:
KARUNA
KITARO'S WORLD OF MUSIC
PEACE ON EARTH
SILK ROAD SUITE
TAMAYURA
WORLD OF KITARO, THE

Documentary Soundtracks:
ANCIENT
AN ANCIENT JOURNEY
SILK ROAD JOURNEY SERIES
YAKUSHI-JI

Public Broadcasting Specials:
AN ENCHANTED EVENING
CIRQUE INGENIEUX

Broadway Score:
CIRQUE INGENIEUX

Videos:
AN ENCHANTED EVENING VOL.1
AN ENCHANTED EVENING VOL. 2
BEST OF KITARO
CIRQUE INGENIEUX
HEAVEN and EARTH
JOURNEY to the HEART
KITARO COLLECTION
KOJIKI
LIGHT OF THE SPIRIT
LIVE IN AMERICA
MILLENNIA, aka Queen Millenia
PEACE ON EARTH
SILK ROAD JOURNEY SERIES
TAMAYURA
THINKING of YOU
YAKUSHI-JI